Getting Started in Coarse Fishing

Tackle, methods and baits
for all waters and species

PAUL DUFFIELD

Copyright © 2017 Paul Duffield

All rights reserved.

ISBN-10: 1976408431
ISBN-13: 978-1976408434

CONTENTS

INTRODUCTION	1
FISHING TACKLE	3
GENERAL ADVICE	21
FISHING METHODS	29
STILL WATER FISHING	35
LOCATING FISH IN STILL WATERS	36
FLOAT RIGS FOR STILL WATERS	37
POLE RIGS FOR STILL WATERS	49
LEGER AND SWIMFEEDER RIGS FOR STILL WATERS	51
LEGER RIGS FOR CARP FISHING	55
RIVER FISHING	60
LOCATING FISH IN RIVERS	61
FLOAT RIGS FOR RIVERS	62
LEGER AND SWIMFEEDER RIGS FOR RIVERS	69
FISHING FOR PREDATORY FISH	74
RIGS FOR PREDATOR FISHING	76
KNOW YOUR COARSE FISH	82
ANATOMY	82
SPECIES IDENTIFICATION	82
BARBEL	83
BREAM	84
CARP	85
CATFISH	86
CHUB	87
CRUCIAN CARP	88
DACE	89
EEL	90
GRAYLING	91
GUDGEON	92
ORFE	93
PERCH	94
PIKE	95
ROACH	96
RUDD	97
TENCH	98
ZANDER	99
OTHER SPECIES	100
KNOW YOUR BAITS	102
POPULAR COARSE FISHING BAITS	102
ARTIFICIAL BAITS	104
LIVE AND DEAD BAITS	105
LURES	105
USEFUL KNOTS	107
KNOTS FOR MAKING LOOPS	107
KNOTS FOR JOINING LINE	108
KNOTS FOR HOOKS AND SWIVELS	109
OTHER KNOTS	111
LICENSES AND PERMISSION TO FISH	112
ABOUT THE AUTHOR	114

INTRODUCTION

I published my first book *The Beginner's Guide to Coarse Fishing* in 2010 and since then have published several other books on fishing and the countryside.

This book incorporates material from my earlier works and is an updated and expanded introductory guide for anyone who has recently taken up coarse fishing, or is thinking of giving it a try.

I wrote in my original book that a good way to start if you want to develop angling as a lifelong hobby is to be an all-rounder, an angler who fishes many different waters and styles to catch a variety of different species of fish.

Nowadays there is even more specialisation in angling, but I still believe that being an all-rounder is the best way to develop a solid grounding in the angling craft.

My intention, in writing this guide is to give you the basic information you need to get started in coarse fishing by covering many different styles of fishing for a wide variety of fish in different types of waters.

PAUL DUFFIELD

FISHING TACKLE

As your angling career develops you may find that the waters you fish, or the type of fishing you prefer, naturally suggest the purchase of more specialised tackle, but if you equip yourself with the items described in this chapter, you will have all you need to begin catching most species of fish in most fishing situations.

FISHING RODS

There are many fishing rods to choose from. In this section I will give some recommendations for rods suitable for the fishing situations a beginner to coarse fishing will encounter.

FLOAT FISHING RODS

To cover a wide range of float fishing situations I suggest that you buy a general purpose float fishing rod of about 12 feet (3.6 metres) in length. If you are small of stature, or are buying equipment for a child, one of about 10 feet (3 meters) may be a better choice to start with as it will be more manageable.

Avoid telescopic rods and specialist rods designed for short range carp fishing, sometimes described as 'stalking rods' as these are not versatile enough to cover a wide range of fishing situations.

When considering the purchase of a float rod, take particular care to ensure that it is made of 'carbon' or 'carbon composite' sometimes referred to just as 'composite'. These rods should be light enough to hold for long periods, whereas cheaper rods made of 'fibreglass' or described as of 'glass' construction will be heavier and are much harder to learn to fish with.

LEGER FISHING RODS

For legering you will usually be able to manage with a shorter rod than needed for float fishing, and I would suggest a rod of between 8.5 feet (2.6 meters) and 10 feet (3 metres) with a range of push in quivertips. Don't worry about what 'quivertips' are for now, I will explain these in the section on techniques later.

Suitable rods will be described as 'leger rods', 'feeder rods' or 'quiver tip rods' and good rods of both 'carbon' and 'carbon composite' material are available at reasonable prices but leger rods are not held for long periods of time, so a 'fibreglass' or 'glass' rod whilst being heavier, will be fine if your budget is restricted.

POLES AND WHIPS

Pole fishing is a method of fishing that does not involve a reel, using a longer 'rod' to which the line is attached to the end. Whip fishing is similar, but with a shorter 'rod' and is a method for catching small fish close to the bank.

It is not necessary to own a pole or a whip to catch fish, a float rod will catch fish in the conditions that a pole or a whip will, but as whips can be obtained very cheaply, and whip fishing is a very easy and enjoyable method of catching small fish that are close to the bank.

If you are planning to teach a child to fish, whip fishing is fishing at its simplest, and is a good way to obtain all you need for a fishing trip for a small outlay.

RODS FOR LARGER FISH

If you intend to try your hand at catching larger fish such as pike, carp or large river barbel, you will need a stronger rod than described earlier.

Although there are specialist rods for each of these species, you can certainly catch pike on a carp rod and carp on a pike rod, and a rod suitable for either of these species will be suitable for legering the larger rivers for barbel.

A good compromise that will be suitable for all three species will be described as a 'specialist' or 'big fish' rod, and will be described as having a 'test curve', a technical term used to describe the amount of weight required to bend the rod through 90 degrees.

A rod of 12 feet (3.6 metres) with a test curve of about 1.75 to 2lb will cover most situations when fishing for these larger specimens, including 'spinning', a general term used for predator fishing with artificial baits for predators such as pike.

GETTING STARTED IN COARSE FISHING

FISHING REELS

As with rods, it is possible to manage with only one reel, but if you do, I suggest that you get one with a spare spool so you can load it with different strengths of line.

There are different types of reel, but for a beginner a reel of the 'fixed spool' type is best. Perfectly good fixed spool reels can be bought for about £5 or £6, and if you can afford it, I suggest that you buy two, preferably with a spare spool each.

You will see reels described as being for 'match fishing', 'legering', 'carp fishing' and so on, but any fixed spool reel in the price range above will be perfectly adequate to start with. You will probably find it easier to begin with if you buy two identical reels, and as this means the spools containing the line will be interchangeable, you will have more options too.

FISHING NETS

There are two types of nets used by coarse anglers; landing nets and keep nets.

LANDING NETS

A landing net should be regarded as a necessity as any fish over a few ounces in weight will be difficult to land without one.

There are many sizes and types of landing net, but when you are starting out, pretty much any landing net of about 24 inches (60cm) measured across the widest part will be suitable, with a handle of about 8 feet (2.5 metres).

Check the rules of the waters you intend to fish before buying a net, as some will insist that you have a landing net of at least a minimum size before you are allowed to fish for carp or pike. If you are intending to fish such waters, you will need to obtain two landing nets as the larger nets for carp and pike fishing are not suitable for general coarse fishing.

You can usually buy nets and handles together for £10 or less, and an alternative to the type with a removable handle is the 'flip up' type of net used by game anglers which are perfectly usable for coarse fishing, but make sure you get one with a long enough handle as many of these have short handles designed for use when wading and will not be suitable if you need to fish from a high bank above the water.

KEEP NETS

A keep net is used to retain fish in the water until you have finished fishing and is optional, only being required if you are intending to fish competitions, or want to be able to look at the fish you have caught at the end of a session. Many commercial fisheries do not allow the use of keep nets, and may restrict their use for larger fish such as carp.

If you do decide to buy a keep net, make sure it is at least 8 feet (2.5 metres) long and complies with the rules set by the environment agency and any waters you intend to fish.

FISHING LINE

You will need line for your reels and also for constructing hook lengths. Hook lengths will be explained later in this guide in the section on fishing techniques.

LINE FOR REELS

Depending on how many reels and spools you buy, you can load your reels with a range of line strengths. Line choice depends on the conditions and the size and type of fish you expect to catch in a given situation, so carrying a selection is advisable.

If you only have two spools a line of 3lbs (1.4 kg) is suitable for a wide range of float fishing situations, and one of 5lbs (2.3 kg) is suitable for most legering situations.

If you have more than two spools, I would suggest you also load one with line of about 10lbs (4.5 kg) and another with line of 4lb (1.6 kg) or 6lb (2.7 kg) if you are mainly intending to use general fishing techniques to catch a range of fish, or 15lb ((6.8 kg) if you are intending to fish where there are very large specimens of carp or pike.

There are many manufacturers of line, and the price can vary widely, but inexpensive line is fine to begin with and will usually be more forgiving in use than the more expensive specialist lines.

You will need 100 metres of line in each of the strengths that you choose to load your reels with and any line described as 'monofilament' or 'nylon' in strengths approximating those above will be fine.

LINE FOR HOOK LENGTHS

It is usual to attach the hook to a line of slightly weaker than that attached to the reel, so that in the event of the line breaking either due to an unexpectedly large fish, or by being caught on an obstruction either in our out of the water, only the short length of line attached to the fish will be lost, resulting in less tackle lost or left attached to a fish.

You will see lines for sale described as for 'hook lengths' but in practice any line that is suitable as reel line will be suitable for hook lengths. In general a hook length of .5 lb (.23 kg) to 1lb (.45 kg) lighter than the reel line will be suitable, so the lines you buy for your reels will determine the additional lines you need to buy for hook lengths.

FISHING FLOATS

If you look at the floats on offer in a fishing tackle shop you will see that there is a huge variety of floats designed to cover every imaginable fishing situation.

You do need a variety of floats if you plan to fish a range of different waters, but a few basic patterns and sizes will be sufficient to begin with.

I will cover float choice for different waters and conditions in more detail later, but in this section I will describe the floats you will need to buy depending on the types of waters you intend to fish.

I will divide these into two broad categories, floats for stillwaters such as lakes, ponds and canals and floats for rivers. If you intend to fish both still and running water you will need a selection from both categories, otherwise you will just need a range of floats from the category for the type of water you intend to fish.

FLOATS FOR STILLWATERS

Most still water floats are collectively known as wagglers. These are straight floats with variations such a thinner section of material inserted at the tip (insert wagglers) or a body of cork, balsa or polystyrene near the base (bodied wagglers).

Waggler floats are usually attached to the line at the bottom only, locked in place by shot. Examples of shotting patterns for these floats will be covered in detail later.

A range of insert wagglers in lengths from 5 to 9 inches (12 to 23cm) carrying shot between 2AAA and 6AAA will cover most still water angling situations. Complete your still water float collection with a few more floats covering the variations described below and you will be well equipped for most stillwaters.

INSERT WAGGLER

A sensitive float usually made from cane, peacock quill or plastic with a straight or slightly tapered body and incorporating a tip of thinner material inserted into the main float body.

BODIED INSERT WAGGLER

A variation on the insert waggler with a body at the base to provide additional stability and shot carrying capacity.

BODIED WAGGLER

A straight float with a body at the base to provide additional stability and shot carrying capacity.

WINDBEATER

A variation on the bodied waggler with a large sight tip to aid visibility when fishing at extreme range. The large sight tip also allows this float to be fished over-depth as it is not easily pulled under by surface tow. This float is sometimes called a driftbeater.

PELLET WAGGLER

The pellet waggler is a thicker and shorter version of the straight waggler developed for fishing in commercial carp fisheries.

LOADED PELLET WAGGLER

A self-cocking version of the pellet waggler developed for fishing in commercial carp fisheries.

BAGGING WAGGLER

The bagging waggler is a version of the pellet waggler than incorporates a cage around which groundbait can be moulded to feed the swim each time the float is cast.

SPLASHER WAGGLER

The splasher waggler is a specialised version of the pellet waggler developed for use on commercial carp fisheries.

MUSHROOM WAGGLER

The mushroom waggler is a specialised version of the pellet waggler developed for use on commercial carp fisheries.

CARP CONTROLLER

The carp controller is used for fishing a bait on the surface, primarily when fishing for carp.

FLOATS FOR RIVERS

There is some overlap between floats for still water and river fishing. Although floats designed specifically for river fishing will probably be those you use the most, there will be times when a straight or insert waggler will be more suitable.

The majority of floats designed for river fishing are attached to the line using silicon tubing at both the top and bottom of the float. Anglers often refer to this as 'top and bottom' or 'double rubber', the latter phrase being from a time when rubber tubing was used in place of silicon.

Although they are all attached to the line and fished in a similar way, there are many different styles of river float, designed to cope with a wide range of fishing conditions.

I will explain the reasons for choosing a specific type of float in detail later, but for now I will describe the main types of river float and suggest which you should buy to ensure you are equipped for the different situations you will encounter.

STICK FLOAT

Stick floats are the most widely used floats for fishing rivers. These are floats constructed in two parts, the top part being of balsa or polystyrene and the bottom of either cane, plastic or wire.

Generally speaking, the further you need to cast, the larger the float you will use, but a small range of stick floats in four or five sizes will be enough to get you started. Avoid the smallest and largest of this type of float, and obtain a few ranging in size from 4 to 6 inches (10 to 15cm) in length.

BALSA FLOAT

These floats are similar in appearance to stick floats, but are more buoyant as they do not incorporate the heavier material in the base that stick floats do. As they take more shot they are suitable for faster water where it is necessary to use a lot of weight to get the bait down to the fish near the bottom.

A range of balsa floats in lengths from 4 to 6 inches (10 to 15cm) will cover most of your angling needs.

AVON FLOAT

These are floats that incorporate a large body of balsa, polystyrene or cork to increase the amount of shot that can be placed on the line. These are mostly used in deeper swims where their extra shot capacity is needed to get the bait down to the fish as quickly as possible.

You will not use these as often as stick floats and balsas, but it is useful to have two or three just in case. A range with shot capacities ranging from 4BB to 6BB will cover most eventualities.

CHUBBER FLOAT

The chubber float is basically a version of the balsa float that is scaled up in width but not length. They carry a much larger amount of shot than a balsa float and are designed primarily to be used with large baits such as lobworms or bread in small and relatively shallow fast flowing rivers.

Unless you intend to specialise in this type of fishing you will rarely, if at all, need to use a chubber, but you may want to carry one or two so you are prepared should the need arise.

STRAIGHT WAGGLER

A simple straight float usually made from reed, peacock quill or plastic. Unlike most river floats, the waggler is attached to line only at the bottom. It is typically used if there is a strong downstream wind and also when fishing very slow rivers or if distance casting is required.

In ideal conditions on slower rivers, the insert version of the waggler described in the section on floats for stillwaters may be used to provide greater sensitivity.

SPECI-WAGGLER

A shorter and thicker version of the straight waggler made from balsa. This float has been developed for fishing shallow swims where the extra thickness and buoyancy allows a shorter float to be used than would be the case with a standard straight waggler.

QUILL FLOATS

Before the development of stick and balsa floats, anglers fished with floats made from bird and porcupine quills. Avon floats incorporating a quill stem are still popular with many anglers and other quill floats can, if you prefer to fish traditionally, be used instead of stick and balsa floats.

As a general guide, floats made from porcupine quill and thin bird quills can be used in place of stick floats, while floats made from thicker quills such as goose and swan can be used in place of balsa and chubber floats.

PACEMAKER AND BIG STICK

You may see variations of the stick and balsa floats described as pacemakers and big sticks. Pacemakers are essentially a thinner version of the balsa while big sticks are thicker bodied versions of the stick float.

Both are useful and effective floats, but if you have a good range of stick and balsa floats you will usually have a float suitable to use in any of the conditions pacemakers and big sticks are designed for.

SHOT

Shot is attached to the line to provide weight to partially sink a float, and can also be used to prevent a leger weight from sliding down the line.

In the past, pieces of lead shot that were manufactured for shotgun cartridges were split to allow them to be pinched on the line, hence the term 'split shot'. Nowadays the use of lead except in the very smallest of sizes is illegal in the U.K., so shot is now manufactured specifically for angling purposes using non-toxic alternatives to lead.

You will need shot in a range of sizes, but the sizes most commonly used are SSG, AAA, BB, number 1, number 4, number 6 and number 8. You should have no trouble obtaining a single 'dispenser' containing a selection of each of these sizes for about £5.

LEGER WEIGHTS

Leger weights are attached to the line to allow a bait to be presented on or near the bed of a river or lake. You will need a range of sizes to cover differences in river flow and the distance you need to cast.

There are many types of leger weight, but the most versatile and the only one you need to begin with is a pear shaped weight incorporating a swivel, known as the Arlesey bomb. Obtain a selection of these in weights from .25 to 1 oz, (7 to 28 grams).

SWIMFEEDERS

Swimfeeders are devices that take the place of leger weights and incorporate a means of getting free offerings of your hook bait or groundbait to the place where you are fishing.

Broadly speaking there are two types, those than are closed at both ends and are mostly used for delivering maggots to the swim and those that are open at both ends and are used to deliver a mix of groundbait (explained later) and maggots, pellets or other baits.

Swimfeeders are not essential to fishing, but if your budget will stretch to it, buy a few of both types in the medium sizes of about 1.5 to 2 inches (3.5 to 5 cm) in length.

HOOKS

You will need different sizes of hooks to suit the different baits and species of fish you are intending to catch.

There are many kinds of hooks made in different gauges of wire, both with and without eyes, with and without barbs, and available loose for tying yourself, or already attached to line.

Hook sizes are described using a numerical scale, the higher the number meaning the smaller the hook. This is variable, though, and different manufacturers seem to apply their own rules about how big a hook should be for a given size.

Over time you will find that you need specialised hooks to suit the types of fishing that you do. For now, though, a few sizes and styles will be versatile enough to cover the various fishing situations you encounter, and a range of hooks of sizes 20, 18, 16, 14, 12, 10 and 8 will be enough to get you started.

Barbless hooks are better when you are starting out learning to handle fishing equipment competently as they are easier to remove from fish, nets and clothing than barbed ones.

Initially the pattern of hook you choose is not too important and a range described as general purpose medium wire hooks will be versatile enough to cover most of your fishing.

By all means buy hooks already tied to line if you prefer and can afford it, but for maximum flexibility loose hooks are better as you can then tie them to various strengths of line.

Loose hooks are available both with eyes, and with 'spade' ends. The former can be tied quite easily by hand, whilst the latter are best tied using a tying aid, usually described as a 'matchman's hook tyer'. Eyed hooks, or those already attached to line may suit you best, as you may feel that you have enough to learn and master already without having to learn to use a hook tying device.

BAIT BOXES

For live baits such as maggots and worms a box is necessary and this needs to have small holes to allow for air flow.

Plastic bait boxes are inexpensive and available in a range of sizes. One or two with a capacity of two to three pints will be fine to begin with.

ROD RESTS

Rod rests are used to provide a convenient place to put the rod when it is not being held in the hand. When legering or still water float fishing the rod will spend a lot of time in the rests, while for running water fishing they provide a safe and convenient place to put the rod when re-baiting or unhooking a fish.

Rod rests are available either with a male thread to allow them to be screwed into bank sticks, or as a single unit incorporating a v shaped rest, and a metal pole to be pushed into the river bank.

If you are on a very tight budget, the single construction type will suffice, but the screw-in type are generally better and more versatile.

For float fishing it is convenient to have both a front rest and a back rest, especially when still water fishing. For legering you may need both a front rest and a back rest, or just a front rest if you need to point the rod into the air, such as when fishing at range on fast flowing rivers.

BANK STICKS

These are metal poles with a spike at one end and a female threaded section at the other. They are used for both rod rests and keep nets. If you obtain rod rests of the screw-in type, or are intending to use a keep net they are essential, otherwise they are not needed.

GENERAL FISHING ITEMS

To complete your kit you can also obtain a number of additional items, some necessary, some optional. Those described here are by no means a comprehensive list, but cover the basics.

The following items fall into the category of 'essential' or 'highly desirable' fishing equipment.

PLUMMETS

These are small weighted devices incorporating either a strip of cork or a hinge to hold the hook while lowering the tackle into the swim to check the depth. These are inexpensive items, and it is useful to have a few as they are easily lost or mislaid when you need them.

FLOAT CAPS

As explained in the section on river floats, you will need some plastic or silicon tubing in various thicknesses to attach floats to the line. These are described as 'float caps' or 'float rubbers' the latter because they were made of rubber before modern materials were available.

You can either buy a packet of pre-cut tubing in mixed sizes, or obtain lengths of plastic or silicon tubing to cut to size when needed.

FLOAT ADAPTERS

These are devices designed to slip over the bottom of 'bottom-only' floats so that if you want to change to a different float during a session you can do so without having to take everything apart.

They are not an essential item by any means as most floats will incorporate a ring for attaching them to the line, but they can save time if a change in conditions means you need to use a heavier float, and they are quite inexpensive.

Some are moulded in one piece from silicon or plastic, and others incorporate a swivel. I've never found much difference in use, so either will do, but it is advisable to get some in different sizes to accommodate different thicknesses of float.

LEGER STOPS

These are designed to be used to prevent a leger weight or swimfeeder from sliding all of the way down the line to the hook. An alternative method is to pinch a piece of shot on the line. Personally I don't find them necessary, while others swear by them as they believe they are less likely to damage fine line. The choice is yours, but if you're on a tight budget they are not essential.

SWIVELS

Swivels are devices that are attached to the line in some situations to prevent the line twisting and in some long distance casting situations they can help to avoid tangles. Having a few in your tackle box can be useful, but they are not essential for most general coarse fishing.

They are relatively cheap, and available in a wide range of sizes. For coarse fishing you don't need the very large or very small ones and a few of about 5 to 6 mm will cover those situations where you may need them.

SPECIALISED FISHING ITEMS

There are many specialised items that can be purchased, and whilst not necessarily essential these may be useful.

BEADS

Hard beads made of plastic, and soft beads made of rubber or silicon can be useful in constructing rigs for legering.

SILICON TUBING

Silicon tubing is sometimes used in rig construction as well as for attaching floats to line.

HAIR RIG STOPS

These are small 'pegs' used to anchor a bait to the line using a 'hair rig'. A hair rig is a term used to describe a tackle arrangement where the bait is not attached to the hook itself, but to a 'hair' of line or other material. At one time hair rigs were only used for carp fishing, but they are now popular for other species such as barbel.

BAIT BANDS

These are silicon bands available in a range of sizes that can be used to attach hard baits such pellets, or large baits such as bread flake to the hook.

BAITING NEEDLE

If you intend to use hair rigs a baiting needle with a small hook near the point will be needed to thread baits such as boilies or soft pellets on to the 'hair'.

TACKLE FOR FISH CARE

There are some items of fishing tackle that you will need to care for the fish to catch. Some fisheries and clubs insist that you are in possession of some of these items before you are allowed to fish.

DISGORGER

This item, which is used to safely remove hooks from fish when they have been swallowed and cannot be removed by hand is an essential item. Disgorgers can be purchased for a few pence each, and you should buy several as they can easily be mislaid. The plastic or nylon variety are best as they will not damage fish. Avoid any that are made of metal and have sharp edges or spikes.

UNHOOKING MAT

This is used to provide a soft cushioned surface on which to unhook fish. Many fisheries where larger fish are expected insist on an unhooking mat, so check the rules to determine whether you need one.

An unhooking mat is not an essential item of tackle if you are not intending to target larger fish, but if you do catch a large fish that cannot be held safely while unhooking, always make sure you unhook it on a soft cushioned surface to avoid damage if the fish 'jumps' around. If you do not have an unhooking mat, leaving the fish in the landing net and placing it on top of a folded jacket while unhooking will protect the fish from being damaged by a hard bank.

ANTISEPTIC

Many fisheries where large expensive carp are the quarry will insist that you use an antiseptic after unhooking fish. Check the rules to see if this is required where you intend to fish.

FORCEPS

Metal forceps can be useful for removing hooks that are not easy to remove by hand and are available quite inexpensively. Not essential, but a useful addition to your fishing kit if your budget allows.

LUGGAGE AND SEATING

When fishing you will need something to sit on and there are a number of specialised chairs and combined seat and tackle carriers available.

What you choose depends on both your budget and the type of fishing you intend to do, but to begin with a stool incorporating a rucksack or one of the rectangular plastic seat boxes will be fine.

Whatever you choose, remember that you will have to carry it to the bank, so something light and compact that is just big enough to accommodate your fishing tackle and some food or drink will be preferable to an unnecessarily large specialised tackle carrier.

You may also wish to purchase a rod holdall to carry your rods, bank sticks and net pole. You can manage without one to begin with, but basic holdalls are inexpensive and make it less of a chore to carry your tackle over long distances. Before you buy a rod holdall make sure that it is long enough to take your longest rod.

CLOTHING FOR FISHING

There is no need to buy specialist angling clothing unless you want to 'look the part'.

It is best to avoid bright colours as you do not want to be any more visible to the fish than you can, but apart from that any outdoor clothing will be suitable.

You will be outside and not moving around a great deal for quite long periods, so make sure that you have sufficient clothing to be warm, and to keep dry if it rains.

In winter, it is best to wear several layers of thin clothing to trap warm air, rather than a single layer of thick clothing. Take care also to ensure that there are no gaps, such as a shirt pulling out of your trousers, as this will create 'cold spots' that are uncomfortable and can result in a lowering of body temperature. A hat is recommended, both for warmth in winter, and so that the peak of a cap, or brim of a hat can shade your eyes from the sun in summer.

Waterproof boots or shoes are also advisable, and in winter it is a good idea to wear an additional pair of thick socks as your feet can become very cold if you are sitting still for long periods of time.

UMBRELLA

An umbrella will be useful if you intend fishing in all weathers and will be fishing in a single swim for the day, rather than adopting a roving approach, when you will want to be 'travelling light'.

Specialist fishing umbrellas are available with metal spikes allowing them to be driven into the ground for stability. Prices vary, and some specialist umbrellas are very expensive, but an inexpensive version will do the job until you can afford something better.

GENERAL ADVICE

This section of the guide contains some general tips and advice that will help you to be more successful with your fishing.

STEALTH TACTICS

When approaching a swim, and while you are tackling up, keep in mind that fish are cautious creatures. They have many predators and are always alert to danger. If you cause disturbance on the bank, or are visible against the skyline, you may spoil your chances of catching fish.

This is particularly important when approaching swims on small rivers, or where the water is very clear.

Tackle up away from the bank side and set up your tackle with the minimum possible disturbance. Just because you cannot see the fish, doesn't mean they cannot see you, and if you can see the fish, they can almost certainly see you.

Make use of bank side cover to hide your presence from the fish. That doesn't just mean cover in front of you – positioning yourself in front of a bank side feature such as a high bank, bush or tree behind you will disguise you, especially if you wear drab clothing that helps you to blend in.

LOADING LINE ON TO A REEL

Line should be loaded on to the reel so that it almost reaches the edge of the spool. A reel that is not loaded with enough line will be difficult to cast with, and reasonable distances will be hard to achieve.

Some reels have narrow spools that only need 100 metres of line to fill them, but others have deep spools and these need to be loaded with backing before attaching the fishing line. You can buy specialist backing, but any old line will do to fill out a spool if you have some.

An alternative to using backing or old line is to wrap self-adhesive tape around the spool, but if you do this, make sure that you apply the tape uniformly so the line will wind evenly on the spool.

ASSEMBLING A ROD

To anyone who has fished for any length of time, this piece of advice will seem so obvious that it hardly needs saying, but in my experience, unless told, many new Anglers just don't think about it.

Many rods are made in three sections and have to be assembled before fishing. This involves pushing the different sections together and lining up the rod rings.

It is much easier to assemble the two thinnest sections first, and then connect these to the thickest or butt section, than assembling the two thickest sections first, as it avoids you having to 'climb up the rod' to attach the end section!

THREADING LINE THROUGH THE ROD RINGS

When threading line through the rod rings, make sure the bale arm of the reel is open, and the anti-reverse is in the off position.

With long rods you will not be able to reach the reel once you have threaded line through half of the rings and the bale arm may close if a bank side obstruction causes it to flip over or turns the reel handle.

If this happens you should be able to finish threading the rings by gently pulling on the line to cause the reel handle to turn and give line.

Although this may seem unlikely to happen, you will be surprised how often it does!

CASTING TECHNIQUES

GETTING STARTED IN COARSE FISHING

There are two main casting techniques that you will need to master, the overhead cast, and the underarm cast.

There are no hard and fast rules about which cast you should use for a given situation and you will quickly develop your own style, but in general terms you would use the overhead cast when you need to cast a long distance, and the underarm cast when long distance casting is not required, and you are fishing with tackle that could easily tangle if you used an overhead cast, such as a stick float rig.

OVERHEAD CAST

This is probably the easier of the two to learn as timing is less important than with the underhand cast. A poorly timed overhead cast will, unless it is really badly mis-timed, just result in less distance, and a bigger splash when the tackle hits the water.

To begin the cast, let out enough line so that you can comfortably swing the tackle by moving the rod backwards and forwards. Open the bail arm of the spool so that the line can run off, and prevent this by trapping the line against the spool with your finger.

Next, lift the rod to a vertical position so that it is pointing straight up. The next part requires practice to get the timing just right so don't worry if your initial attempts don't go too well.

Imagine that you are standing next to a large clock face, and the rod is currently pointing to 12 o'clock.

In one fluid movement, swing the tackle behind you by moving the rod sharply back so that it is pointing at between 10 and 11 o'clock, and then immediately move the rod sharply forwards so that it is pointing at between 1 and 2 o'clock. Stop the rod, and release the line by lifting your finger off the spool.

If you get the timing right, the tackle should be propelled away from you towards the place where you want to fish, and if the spool is loaded correctly, line should come off the spool freely.

When the tackle is a few inches above the water, drop the rod tip to between 3 and 4 o'clock, and the tackle should land gently on the surface without causing too much disturbance.

The most difficult part of the cast is timing the release of the line correctly. If you release too early, the line will fly up in the air without the necessary power, and will land in a heap. Release too late, and the tackle will not achieve the required distance and will be driven with excessive force into the water.

UNDERHAND CAST

This cast will not achieve the same distance as the overhead cast, but it does give you more control over the tackle in flight, and is less likely to result in the tackle becoming tangled.

To begin the cast, assuming you are right handed, hold the rod in your right hand, open the bail arm of the reel, and let out enough line from the rod tip so that with your left hand you can comfortably hold the line just above the hook.

Hold the rod across your body while keeping the line under tension with your left hand, and then flick the rod towards the water so that it is pointing directly away from you, at the same time releasing the line held in your left hand. You should find that the tackle is propelled towards the place you want to fish, and if you get enough power into the cast, and get your timing right, line should flow off the spool.

Timing of this cast is quite difficult to master, but with practice you will find that it becomes second nature. As your skills progress you will find that you can achieve this cast holding the rod at different angles to avoid bank side vegetation and other obstacles.

STRIKING OR SETTING THE HOOK

Striking is the term used to describe the action of setting the hook in the fish when you get a bite.

It is not usually necessary to do more than move the rod swiftly back a few inches with a flick, but when fishing at range, or if there is a lot of slack line between you and your tackle, you may need to strike with a sweeping action to pick up the slack line and make contact with the fish.

Speed of the strike is much more important than power as all you are trying to do is pull the hook firmly into the mouth of the fish before it has time to eject the bait.

As a general rule, keep in mind that the closer in you are fishing, the less powerfully you need to strike.

An unnecessarily powerful strike when fishing at close range will result in your tackle being pulled out of the water, sometimes with a small fish attached! There is no surer way that I know of to get your tackle in a tangle!

PLAYING FISH

Small fish can be wound in quite easily and then swung to hand, but large fish are capable of long sustained fights during which you may have to give line.

When you hook a large fish, do not try to bully it out of the water as quickly as possible, your aim is to tire the fish so that when all of the fight has gone out of it, you can draw it safely over the landing net.

Large fish will try to swim away from you as fast as they can when they are hooked, or soon after as they feel resistance. You will usually need to give line to prevent a break or the hook pulling free and this can be done in two ways.

Most reels are equipped with a slipping clutch. This allows the spool to rotate to give line when the pull is approaching that which would break the line. An alternative is to allow the fish to take line under pressure by winding the reel backwards. Personally I prefer to backwind, using judgement to determine when giving line is necessary. If you do choose to use the slipping clutch, make sure it is set to just below the breaking strain of the line. Too slack and you will struggle to recover line, too tight and you risk a break.

Playing a fish is a little like a tug of war match. You give a little, you gain a little until eventually the fish is tired. To gain the maximum advantage from your tackle it is essential that you use the rod to cushion the lunges of the fish, so most of the time you should hold it high. This applies maximum pressure on the fish, and also prevents it from coming too high in the water before it is ready for the net.

The exception to this is when you need to stop a fish from reaching an obstruction such as a weed bed or some tree roots. If you lock down the reel and try to stop the fish by holding the rod high you may pull out the hook or break the line. When you need to stop a fish in this way, drop the rod tip so you are applying 'side strain'. Usually this will force the fish up nearer the surface and is often enough to make it change direction away from the snag.

Learning to play a fish well is something that only experience can teach you, but with perseverance you will develop an instinct for when a fish is ready to be brought to the net.

LANDING FISH

When a fish is tired you will notice that its lunges and runs become weaker and shorter. This can be the most dangerous part of the fight, as the fish will be closer and nearer the surface and you have only a short amount of line between you and the fish.

Very often, a fish that has been brought to the surface will make a desperate lunge for freedom as soon as it sees you or the net, so be prepared to give more line and continue the fight when this happens.

Eventually the fish will be beaten and will turn sideways on the surface. Now is the time to slip the net under the fish and draw it back from the water.

Do not drag the fish for a long distance to the net, try to get the net as close to the fish and draw it over the lip of the net in a steady controlled movement. When fishing fast rivers you may need to position the net a little downstream of the fish, and allow the current to take the fish over the net. Never try to pull a beaten fish against the current as that is a sure way of pulling out the hook.

Once the fish is in the net, draw the net back in the water to ensure the fish is safely in the folds. You should then disengage the bale arm on the reel and place the rod in its rest so you have both hands free to lift the net.

Do not lift the net out of the water while you are still holding the end of the pole as it will bend, and could break. Instead, slide the pole backwards until you can safely lift it out of the water by gripping the pole with both hands near the net.

UNHOOKING FISH

Small fish can be safely unhooked in the hand after being swung in, larger fish should be unhooked while lying on the bank supported on a soft surface such as an unhooking mat.

Be careful when unhooking fish not to grip them too tightly, and only handle them with damp hands to prevent removal of slime.

Most of the time a fish will be hooked in the lip, and the hook can be easily removed by hand. Grip the shank of the hook between finger and thumb and gently pull it out. Barbless hooks will come out easily, but barbed hooks may need to be removed by very gently shaking the hook at the same time as pulling to release the grip of the barb.

If the fish is hooked deeper in the mouth and you cannot reach it with your fingers, you may need to use forceps to grimly grip the hook to remove it using the same technique as above.

USING A DISGORGER

When a fish has swallowed the hook and you cannot see it to grip it with forceps you will need to use a disgorger. You should make sure that you have several of these in your fishing kit and jacket so you can quickly lay your hands on one when needed. Some anglers have a disgorger on a piece of string round their neck, or on a cord attached to their jacket so it is close to hand.

A disgorger is simple to use, but takes a little practice. Keep the line under gentle tension by wrapping it around a finger of the hand that is holding the disgorger. Then, slide the disgorger on to the line using the slot in the side, and gently push the disgorger down the line until you feel the resistance of the hook.

A further gentle push should dislodge the hook, and you should then turn the disgorger by about 25 degrees and pull it back out of the fish. It should come out with no resistance, so if it will not come out easily, the hook has not been dislodged and you need to repeat the process.

RETURNING FISH TO THE WATER

It is important that you do not throw fish back into the water as they are fragile creatures and could be damaged. Instead, gently slip the fish into the water nose first and it should swim away strongly.

On high banks you may not be able to reach the water, so return the fish by lowering it to the surface in your landing net and gently turning it out.

Some fish, notably Barbel, need time to recover before they can swim away and you may need to support them with their noses pointed into the current until you feel them swim away from you.

If you use a keep net, release the fish at the end of the session by gently lifting the end of the net furthest from the mouth so the fish swim out. Do not allow fish to flap around in the bottom of a net out of water as the larger fish will damage themselves, and other smaller fish below them.

If you want to weigh your fish after a session you will need to remove them from the net while it is out of water. Some keep nets have a ring that allows the bottom of the net to be lifted out of the mouth so fish can be removed safely.

If your keep net does not have this feature, move the fish as near to the mouth of the net as possible using the method in the previous paragraph before gently tipping them into the weighing net. The head of a landing net can be used to weigh fish if you do not have a specialist weighing net or basket.

FISHING METHODS

The purpose of this section of the guide is to briefly explain the different methods that you can use to catch fish in a variety of locations. More detail on each type of fishing can be found in the following section describing different fishing rigs.

FLOAT FISHING

Float fishing is a technique where the baited hook is suspended above the bed of the lake, river or canal using a float made of buoyant material. Shot is used to cause the float to 'sit' in the water with only the tip visible above the surface.

A bite is detected by watching for the float to be partially or completely submerged by a biting fish.

FLOAT FISHING ON LAKES AND CANALS

When float fishing on lakes and canals the float is attached to the line at the bottom using shot. This is known as 'bottom only'.

More sensitive floats are required than for river fishing, as the fish alone is responsible for pulling the float down in the water as there is no current, so floats with thin tips, sometimes inserted into a thicker body are used.

The remaining shot required to sink the float so only the tip is showing are then placed on the line between the float and the hook. If you want the bait to sink slowly so that fish feeding up in the water can intercept it, the shot is spaced out, but if you want to get the bait down to the bottom quickly, perhaps because a lot of small fish near the surface are taking the bait before it can reach larger fish below, the shot will be bunched closer to the hook.

After casting the float to the desired fishing spot, the line needs to be sunk so that the float is not dragged around by surface drift or wind. To do this, immediately after casting drop the tip of the rod in the water, and lift it sharply up. This should cause the line between the rod and the float to be pulled beneath the surface. An alternative, if this proves difficult, is to cast beyond the place where you want to fish, and then dip the rod tip in the water, and wind a couple of sharp turns of the reel.

Once the float is in position and the line submerged, the rod should be placed in two rests such that the handle of the rod is conveniently to hand for striking, and the tip is in or near the water to prevent any loose line from being affected by wind.

Watch the float carefully for bites. It may dip quickly under the water, but more often you will see the float dip slightly, move to one side, or even come up in the water. All are signals to strike, which should be done by sharply lifting the rod tip up to set the hook.

When fishing in still-water, the size of float you decide to fish with is determined by the distance you plan to fish at, whether you are casting into a head wind or cross wind and the depth of water.

You should be able to cast comfortably to the place you wish to fish, so if you are finding this difficult or if the wind increases, switch to a larger float or one with a body at the base so you can put more shot on the line. When fishing deep water a larger float may be needed to allow more shot to be placed on the line to get the bait down to the bottom more quickly.

You should always find out the depth using a plummet, and it is usually best to start by fishing on or near the bottom, but if fish are in the upper levels of water you will often get bites 'on the drop' while the baited hook is falling through the water. If the fish are small, you can move the bulk shot nearer the hook to get a faster fall through the water, or even reduce the size of the locking shot to allow more bulk shot to be placed on the line.

If, on the other hand, it is the fish you wish to catch that are feeding up in the water, moving the shot higher up the line and shortening the line between the float and the hook will ensure that your baited hook stays longer in the feeding zone.

Unlike river float fishing it is the fish alone that pulls the float under the surface when you get a bite, so you should use the thinnest tip that conditions allow. The thicker the tip, the more pull a fish needs to exert to pull it under. A thinner tip will be pulled further beneath the surface making bites easier to spot, whereas a thick tip may hardly move, and worse may cause resistance that the fish can feel resulting in it ejecting the bait before you have time to strike.

If you are having trouble hitting bites, it pays to adjust the position of the small 'dropper' shot either nearer to the hook or further away until you find the distance that results in the most bites being hit.

While the tackle is in the water, you will keep the bail arm of the reel closed to prevent line being blow off by wind. Whether you also engage the reel's anti-reverse mechanism is a matter of personal choice. If you do, there is no risk of the strike being cushioned by line being pulled off the reel, but you will need to disengage the anti-reverse to play large fish. If you leave the anti-reverse in the off position you will not have to do this, but you will need to trap the spool of the reel with your finger when striking to prevent line being given when you strike.

FLOAT FISHING ON RIVERS

When float fishing on rivers you will usually attach the float to the line using silicon or plastic tubing placed at both ends of the float. This is known as 'top and bottom' or 'double rubber'.

Shot is then attached to the line between the float and the hook, either spaced out or in bunches so that only the tip of the float is visible above the water.

The tackle is then swung out into the stream and allowed to float down the river with the current.

You need to continually pay put line with this method, so the bale arm of the reel is left open and the line is controlled by pressure applied with your finger at the edge of the spool.

To keep a tight line to the float you may need to 'mend the line' by trapping the line with your finger and lifting the rod until the line between the rod tip and float is straight. On rivers where the flow is slow and there are many surface currents you may need to do this several times on each passage of the float down the swim.

This technique is referred to as 'trotting', and when the float needs to travel a long way down the swim to reach the fish, it is known as 'long trotting'.

When you get a bite, trap the line against the spool with your finger and strike with a sweeping movement away from the float. The further away the float is, the more powerful the strike, but often it is only necessary to stop the float as the current will set the hook.

Another river float fishing method involves the use of a Waggler float that is only attached to the line at the bottom. This allows the float to be cast further without risk of tangles on wide rivers, or when you want to fish near the far bank.

With this method it is not possible to keep a tight line to the float as this would cause it to be pulled towards you and the bait would not appear to be behaving naturally to the fish.

Instead of mending the line, you allow a bow to form between the rod tip and float, and you then 'feed the bow' by paying out enough line to allow the float to move unhindered down the swim.

A more powerful strike is required with this method as you have to recover all of the line in the bow before making contact with the fish. This is achieved by a high sweeping movement of the rod over your shoulder.

With both methods, as soon as a fish is hooked you have to decide whether you need to allow it to take line before you close the bail arm of the reel in preparation for winding in or playing the fish. If it is a small fish you can immediately close the bail arm and commence winding. If you feel resistance from a large fish, allow it to take line with the bail arm open, and close it only when you feel the fish stop its initial run.

When fishing with running line tackle on rivers, make sure that the anti-reverse on the reel is set to the off position if you intend to give line by winding backwards rather than using the slipping clutch.

LEGERING

Legering is a technique where the baited hook is fished on or near the bed of the river, lake or canal by means of a weight that is attached to the line.

A bite is detected by watching the tip of the rod for a pull caused by a biting fish. Bites may also be detected by holding the line between finger and thumb.

LEGERING ON LAKES AND CANALS

When legering on still waters, it is usual to fish with a swimfeeder so that you can introduce ground bait and loose feed into the swim near your bait.

Still water legering is a popular technique for catching Bream which are bottom feeders, but this technique will catch many species of fish, and is sometimes necessary when you need to cast further than is possible with float tackle.

As you will be introducing feed into the swim on every cast, it is important that your tackle always lands in roughly the same area to avoid spreading feed widely over the bottom which would result in the fish not being concentrated where you are fishing.

You will normally use the overhead cast to achieve maximum distance, and the first part of ensuring that your tackle always lands in roughly the same place is to choose a marker on the opposite bank, and cast towards that each time.

When you are first starting out, that is probably all you should concentrate on, relying on judgment to cast approximately the same distance each time, but as you progress, you can use rubber bands or line clips to prevent line from being taken from the spool once you have cast the required distance.

For still water fishing you should use the finest tip that came with your leger rod, and you need to position the rod in two rod rests more or less parallel to the bank, so that an angle of about 90 degrees is formed between the tip of the rod and your tackle. This will give the maximum indication on the tip when you get bites.

After casting out, wait a few seconds after the tackle hits the water to allow the leger or swimfeeder to reach the bottom, and then close the bail arm on the reel. Next position the rod in the rests and take up the slack line so that the line between the rod tip and your tackle is tight.

You are now ready to watch the tip for indications of a bite which make come in the form of a pull or tap, or a slackening of the line caused by a fish picking up the bait and swimming towards you.

When you get a bite, lift the rod out of the rests and strike with a sharp movement of the rod away from the tackle.

If bites are coming slowly you may need to re-cast regularly to get a decent amount of ground bait and loose feed into the swim.

LEGERING ON RIVERS

When legering on slow rivers you can use a similar technique to that described for still water legering. On fast rivers, however, a different method is required.

When the pull of the current is strong, you need to take this into account when deciding the weight of leger or swimfeeder to use. You need to use just enough weight to prevent the tackle being dislodged and carried down the swim.

You will need to use a heavier quivertip than for still water legering as the pull of a strong current will bend a light tip round making bite detection difficult, and you may also need to position the rod in one rest, pointing up at an angle of about 45 degrees to the water to relieve the water pressure on the line which could dislodge your tackle.

When you are ready cast out the tackle as described for still water legering, and allow time for the tackle to reach the bottom before closing the bail arm and positioning the rod in the rest.

You should then take up any slack line, but in some conditions it may be necessary to leave a bow in the line between the tip and the leger or swimfeeder due to the pull of the current.

As with still water legering, bites may come in the form of a pull or slackening of the line, which is your indication to strike. You will find, though, that fish often hook themselves when you are fishing in strong currents, and all that is necessary is for you to lift the rod and begin playing the fish.

STILL WATER FISHING

Still water fisheries come in all shapes and sizes and can contain fish of a wide variety of sizes and species.

COMMON SPECIES

- Bream
- Carp
- Perch
- Pike
- Roach
- Tench

As a general rule, especially on the smaller commercial and day ticket fisheries, a simple waggler or pole setup can be used to fish a short distance from the bank to catch a variety of species including roach, bream, tench and carp.

Larger waters, especially those which are shallow in the margins with deeper water some distance from the bank, require more specialised float fishing or legering techniques to be used.

Targeting the larger specimens of carp, tench or bream requires the use of methods and baits that will avoid the attention of smaller fish that may be present and maximise the chances of catching the target species.

LOCATING FISH IN STILL WATERS

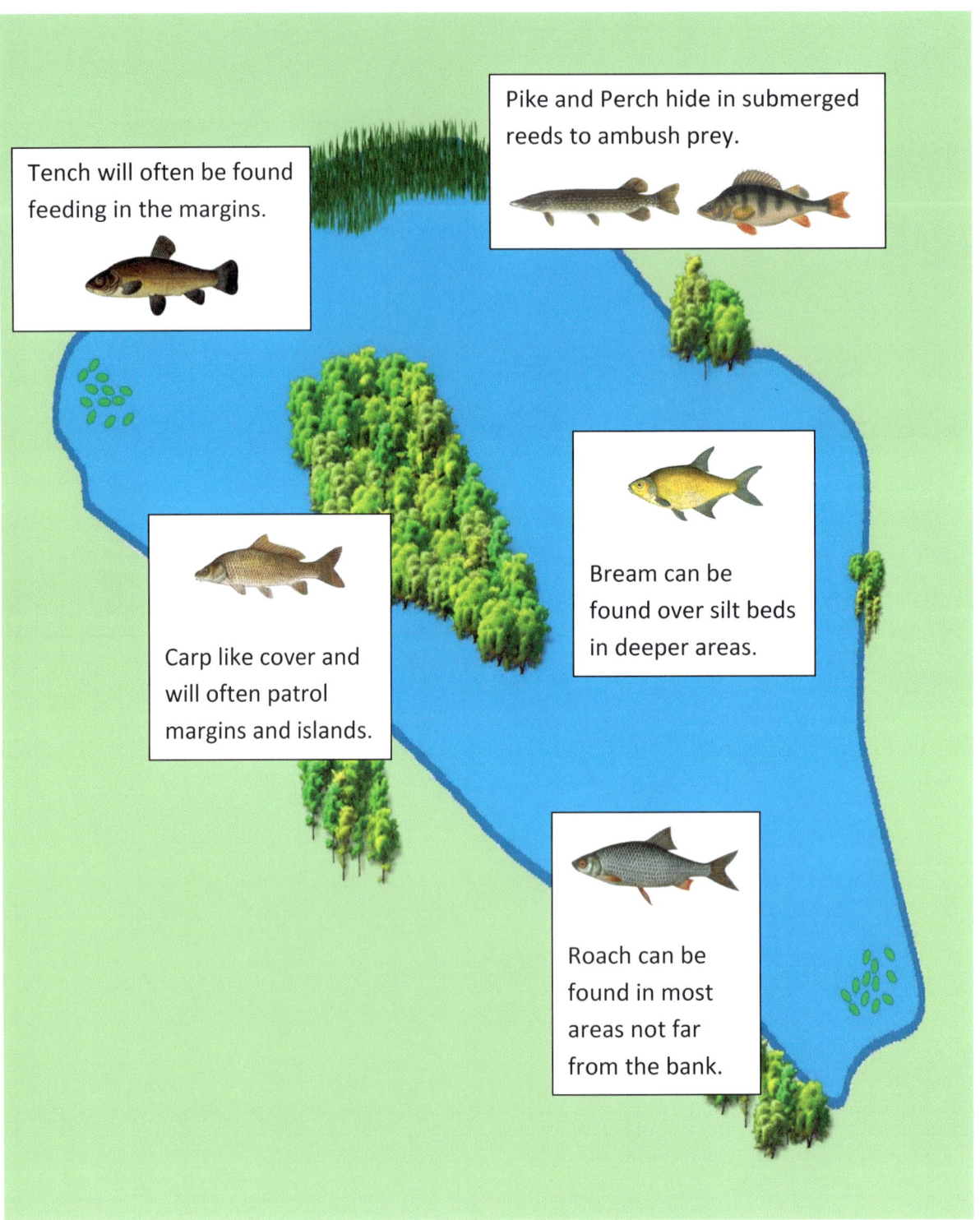

GETTING STARTED IN COARSE FISHING

FLOAT RIGS FOR STILL WATERS

INSERT WAGGLER FLOAT RIG

A sensitive rig that can catch fish at all depths.

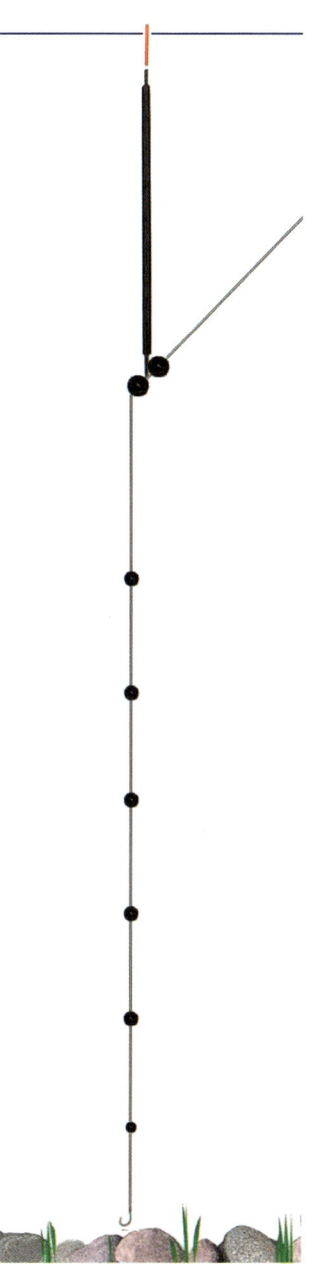

> **HOW TO SET UP THE RIG**
>
> The bulk of the shot required to set the float should be used to lock it on to the line.
>
> Smaller shots, number 6 or number 8, are spaced evenly down the line, finishing with a number 8 or number 10 dropper shot 5 to 10 inches from the hook.

Strike at any indication that the float is not settling in the water.

If bites occur soon after you have cast the float, these will often not result in the float being pulled under, but instead it may move across the surface or appear to have stopped settling.

If you find that you are getting bites only after the float has settled, you can increase the rate at which the hook bait falls by moving the shot nearer the hook.

Similarly, shot can be moved nearer to the float if the fish are feeding higher in the water.

37

BODIED INSERT WAGGLER FLOAT RIG

A sensitive rig for fishing at long range.

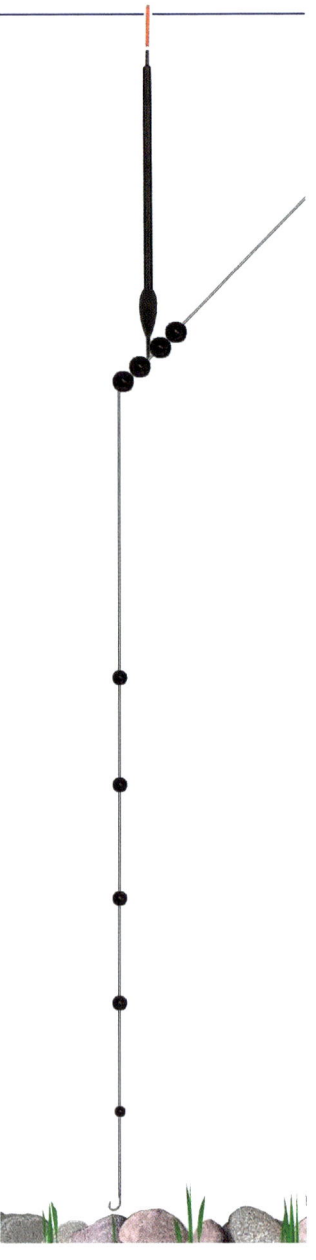

HOW TO SET UP THE RIG

The bulk of the shot required to set the float should be used to lock it on to the line.

Smaller shots, number 6 or number 8, are spaced evenly starting about a third of the way from the float to the hook, finishing with a number 8 or number 10 dropper shot 5 to 10 inches from the hook.

If you find that you are getting bites only after the bait has fallen almost to the bottom of the water, you can increase the rate at which the hook bait falls by moving the shot nearer the hook.

Similarly, shot can be moved nearer to the float if the fish are feeding higher in the water.

BODIED WAGGLER FLOAT RIG

An ideal rig for long range fishing when there is a tow or strong ripple on the water.

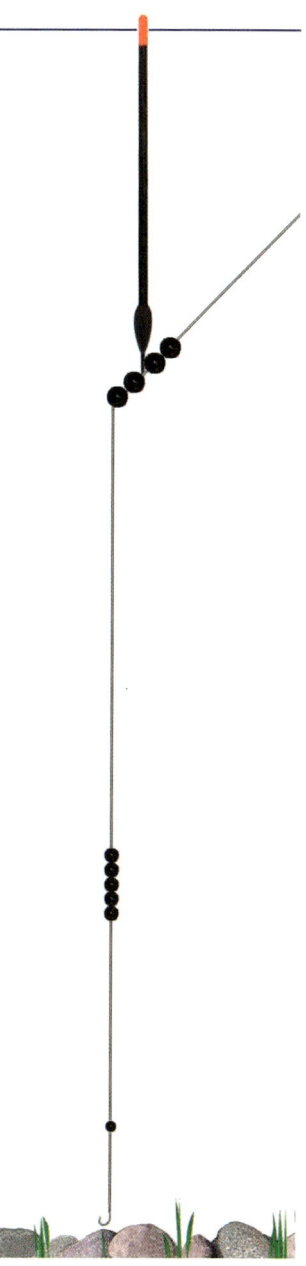

> **HOW TO SET UP THE RIG**
>
> The bulk of the shot required to set the float should be used to lock it on to the line.
>
> Smaller shots, number 6 or number 8, are bulked below half depth finishing with a number 8 or number 10 dropper shot 5 to 10 inches (12 to 25 cm) from the hook.

The thicker tip helps to prevent the float from dragging under when fishing over depth and is more visible than the thinner tip of the bodied insert waggler.

If you find that you are getting bites 'on the drop' the shot can be moved further up the line or spaced out to provide a slower sinking hook bait.

There are occasions when fish are feeding on the bottom and will only take a static bait. If tow is causing the float to drift, this can be overcome by fishing over depth with one or two shots lying on the bottom.

WINDBEATER FLOAT RIG

A rig for fishing a static bait when there is a strong tow.

> **HOW TO SET UP THE RIG**
>
> Attach a single number 1 shot about 9 inches (23 cm) from the hook and lock the float to the line using the remaining shot required so that only the body is submerged and the whole stem sits out of the water.

Plumb the depth and set the float so that 12 inches (30 cm) of line will be lying on the lake bed.

After casting, wait until the bottom shot has reached the bottom, then place the rod in two rests with the tip just under the surface and wind in until only the sight tip of the float is visible above the water.

When a fish moves the bottom shot by taking the bait, the float will rise out of the water which is your signal to strike.

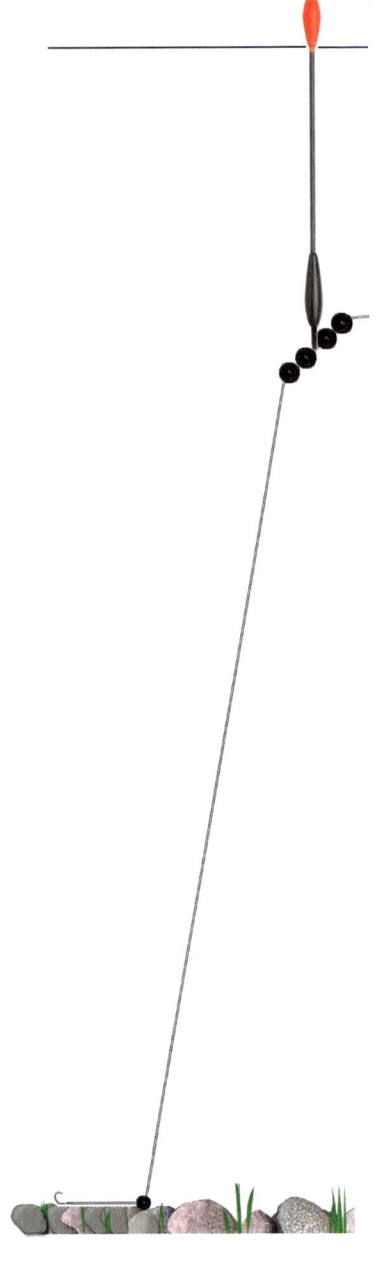

SLIDER FLOAT RIG

A rig for float fishing in very deep swims.

> **HOW TO SET UP THE RIG**
>
> No shot is used around the base of the float, instead the float is free running with a stop knot tied above the float at the depth of the water.
>
> Shotting comprises two number 8 droppers above the hook followed by a large bulk of shot about 3 feet (90 cm) above the hook.
>
> A further number 8 shot is placed on the line above the bulk shot for the float to rest on during casting.

A float with a large shot capacity such as a bodied waggler is required for this method.

If you use a float adapter with this method it will need to be the type with a swivel to ensure the float runs freely on the line.

After casting, wait for the bulk shot to pull through the float eye and settle before closing the bale arm and putting the rod on rests.

LIFT METHOD FLOAT RIG

An effective rig for bottom feeding fish such as tench and bream.

> ### HOW TO SET UP THE RIG
>
> The float is locked on to the line using two small shots. A single shot, large enough to set the float, is placed 2 to 6 inches (5 to 15 cm) from the hook.

The depth must be accurately plumbed so that when the large shot is sitting on the bottom of the water, only the very top of the float is visible.

Bottom feeding fish may not move far after picking up the hook bait, so a bite may not be seen using a standard waggler rig.

When a fish takes the bait, the shot will be lifted off the bottom and the float will come up in the water signaling the bite.

PELLET WAGGLER FLOAT RIG

A rig for fishing near the surface on commercial carp fisheries.

> **HOW TO SET UP THE RIG**
>
> The hook length is attached to the main line using a small swivel to avoid line twist.
>
> All of the shot required to set the float is used to lock it on the line by placing equal numbers of shot either side of the float.

Normally used with hair rigs to fish with banded or drilled pellets as the bait.

As large shots are required, some anglers place thin silicon tubing either side of the float and attach the shot to the tubing to avoid the shot damaging the line.

A depth of around 2 feet (60 cm) is a good starting point, but be prepared to adjust this until you find the depth at which the fish are feeding.

Flicking the rod tip to move the float every 30 seconds or so will lift the bait and cause a disturbance which may induce a bite.

LOADED PELLET WAGGLER FLOAT RIG

A variation on the standard pellet waggler that does not require any shot on the line.

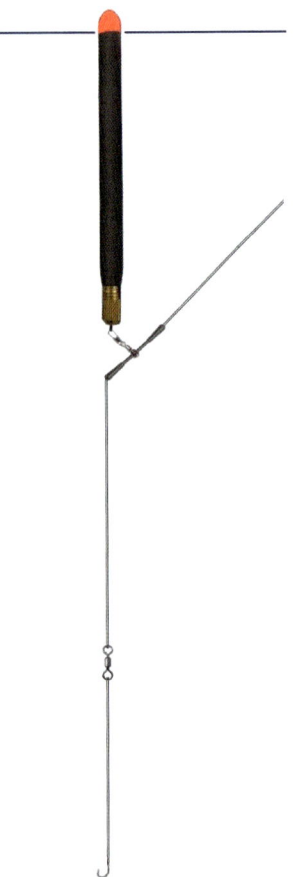

HOW TO SET UP THE RIG

A specialised pellet float adapter is used to lock the float in place.

The hook length is attached to the main line using a small swivel to avoid line twist.

A depth of around 2 feet (60 cm) is a good starting point, but be prepared to adjust this until you find the depth at which the fish are feeding.

Flicking the rod tip to move the float every 30 seconds or so will lift the bait and cause a disturbance which may induce a bite.

SPLASHER WAGGLER FLOAT RIG

A variation on the loaded pellet waggler that is designed to attract carp by maximising the splash when the float lands on the water.

> ### HOW TO SET UP THE RIG
>
> A specialised pellet float adapter is used to lock the float in place.
>
> The hook length is attached to the main line using a small swivel to avoid line twist.

Particularly effective on well stocked commercial carp fisheries where the fish have learned to associate a disturbance on the surface with food.

A depth of around 2 feet (60 cm) is a good starting point, but be prepared to adjust this until you find the depth at which the fish are feeding.

BAGGING WAGGLER FLOAT RIG

A version of the loaded pellet waggler that incorporates a groundbait cage at the base.

> **HOW TO SET UP THE RIG**
>
> A specialised pellet float adapter is used to lock the float in place.
>
> The hook length is attached to the main line using a small swivel to avoid line twist.

A depth of around 2 feet (60 cm) is a good starting point, but be prepared to adjust this until you find the depth at which the fish are feeding.

Each cast, a ball of method mix groundbait incorporating some samples of hook bait, is moulded on to the cage at the base of the float.

A fluffy groundbait mix is required with a consistency that does not stick to the float after it lands in the water, but is stiff enough not to come off during the cast.

GETTING STARTED IN COARSE FISHING

MUSHROOM WAGGLER FLOAT RIG

A version of the loaded pellet waggler designed for fishing at long range.

> **HOW TO SET UP THE RIG**
>
> A specialised pellet float adapter is used to lock the float in place.
>
> The hook length is attached to the main line using a small swivel to avoid line twist.

A flat top is incorporated into the float to counter the tendency of a heavy float to dive under the surface when a powerful cast is required to reach the required distance.

A depth of around 2 feet (60 cm) is a good starting point, but be prepared to adjust this until you find the depth at which the fish are feeding.

CARP CONTROLLER FLOAT RIG

A rig for fishing a floating bait when fish are feeding on the surface.

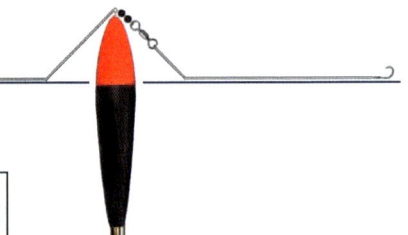

HOW TO SET UP THE RIG

The main line is threaded through the eye at the top of the float, followed by one or two rubber beads that act as a shock absorber.

A size 8 swivel is then tied to the end of the main line and the hook length is tied to the other side of the swivel.

Hair rigged floating baits such as floating pellets and bread work well with this method. Small amounts of feed should be introduced regularly. If you feed too much, wind may carry the excess bait out of your swim, followed by the fish.

Bites are detected either by watching the float for movement or watching the end of the rod tip. Bites are usually aggressive and result in the fish being hooked without the need to strike.

POLE RIGS FOR STILL WATERS

SLOW SINKING POLE RIG

A sensitive rig that can catch fish at all depths.

> **HOW TO SET UP THE RIG**
>
> Small shots, number 6 or number 8, are spaced evenly down the line, finishing with a number 8 or number 10 dropper shot 5 to 10 inches from the hook.

Strike at any indication that the float is not settling in the water.

If you only bites only after the float has settled, increase the rate at which the hook bait falls by moving the shot nearer the hook.

The rig can be shortened to fish off the bottom or shot can be moved nearer to the float if the fish are feeding higher in the water.

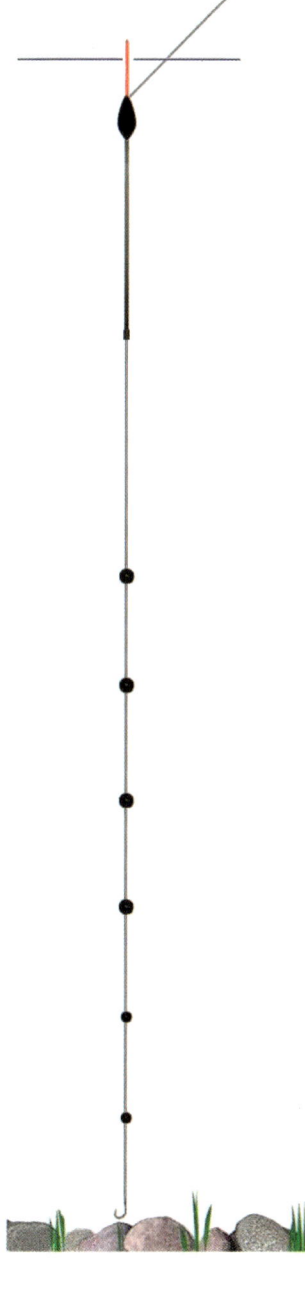

FAST SINKING POLE RIG

A rig for fishing at or near the bottom of the swim.

> ### HOW TO SET UP THE RIG
>
> Small shots, number 6 or number 8, are bulked below half depth finishing with a number 8 or number 10 dropper shot 5 to 10 inches (12 to 25 cm) from the hook.

By bulking the shot below half depth, the bait will fall to the bottom more quickly.

This helps to avoid the attention of smaller fish feeding up in the water if you are targeting larger fish below.

LEGER AND SWIMFEEDER RIGS FOR STILL WATERS

RUNNING LEGER/FEEDER RIG

A simple rig for use with a leger or swimfeeder.

HOW TO SET UP THE RIG

Slide a link swivel on to the main line followed by a leger stop (a small split shot or swivel and bead can be used if you prefer), tie a loop in the main line and attach a hook link of 18 inches (45 cm).

A leger weight or swimfeeder is attached to the rig using the link swivel which gives you the flexibility to switch between leger and feeder, or change to a heavier or lighter leger weight without having to break the rig down.

As the line can pass freely through the eye of the swivel there is little resistance when a fish takes the bait.

SEMI-FIXED LEGER/FEEDER RIG

A semi-fixed version of the running leger rig. It can be very effective when bites are difficult to see because the fish are not moving far after taking your bait.

> ### HOW TO SET UP THE RIG
>
> Slide one or two float stops on to the main line, followed by a link swivel and a leger stop (a small split shot or swivel and bead can be used if you prefer), tie a loop in the main line and attach a hook link of 18 inches (45 cm).

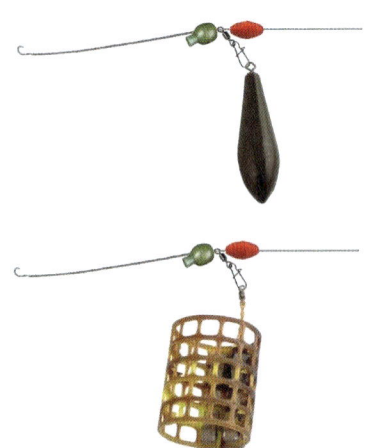

This rig is designed to provide resistance as soon as a fish takes the bait causing it to either swim away quickly and provide a positive indication of a bite, or hook itself against the weight of the leger or feeder.

PATERNOSTER FEEDER RIG

A very sensitive rig that shows up bites very well as any movement of the hook is quickly transmitted up the line to the rod tip.

HOW TO SET UP THE RIG

Slide one or two float stops on to the main line followed by swivel and a soft bead. Tie another swivel to the end of the main line and attach 10 inches (25 cm) of line to the other end of the swivel.

The leger or swimfeeder is tied to the end of this line and an 18 inch (45 cm) hook link is attached to the swivel between the bead and the float stop. Use the float stop to lock the hook length swivel in place.

Experiment with longer or shorter hook links if you have difficulty seeing or hitting bites.

INLINE FEEDER RIG

A semi-fixed rig, designed to provide resistance as soon as a fish takes the bait causing it to either swim away quickly and provide a positive indication of a bite, or hook itself against the weight of the feeder.

HOW TO SET UP THE RIG

Thread one or two floats stops on to the line, followed by the feeder and tie a swivel to the end of the main line.

Tie a very short hook link of about 3 inches (8 cm) to the other end of the swivel and push the float stop up to the feeder to lock everything in place.

The combination of a very short hook link and inline feeder makes this a very easy rig to cast quite long distances without tangles.

The reason for the short hook link is twofold. Firstly it ensures that your hook bait is among the maggots escaping from the feeder.

Secondly, it means that a fish will feel the resistance of the swimfeeder as soon as they take the bait which should result in a positive bite or hooked fish.

LEGER RIGS FOR CARP FISHING

SEMI-FIXED SAFETY BOLT RIG

A safe version of the bolt rig, designed to provide resistance as soon as a fish takes the bait causing it to either run, providing positive indication of a bite, or hook itself against the weight of the leger.

> **HOW TO SET UP THE RIG**
>
> Thread the main line through a tail sleeve and safety clip and attach a swivel to the end of the main line.
>
> Push the swivel into the safety clip, attach a weight and push the sleeve over the end of the clip.
>
> Complete the rig by tying a hair link hook length to the swivel.

If the leger becomes snagged when playing a fish it will break free from the safety clip. In the event of a break off, either the swivel will pull free from the safety clip or the leger will pull free to ensure that the fish is not tethered to the leger.

If you prefer not to use a safety clip, a similar rig can be constructed by threading the swivel directly on to the mainline, with a float stop and swivel either side.

HELICOPTER RIG

One of the earliest specialist carp rigs designed for long range tangle free casting. It is so named because the hook link revolves around the main line during the cast.

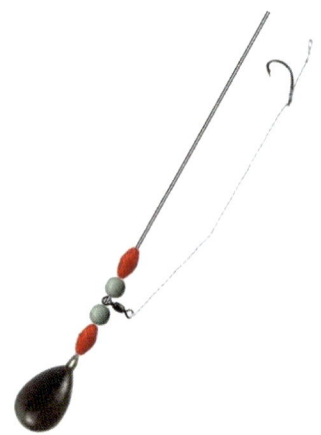

HOW TO SET UP THE RIG

Thread a float stop on to the line, followed by a bead, a swivel, another bead and another float stop.

A leger is tied to the end of the main line and a hair rig hook link to the swivel. Push the float stops, beads and swivel down to the leger to lock everything in place but make sure that the swivel can move freely around the main line.

There are many variants of the helicopter rig and many companies have developed components specifically for its construction, but a simple version of this rig can be easily constructed using basic coarse fishing tackle.

Some anglers prefer to construct this to rig using tubing pushed through the beads, dispensing with the float stops, or with specialised rig components.

CHOD RIG

A variant of the helicopter rig designed to be fished with a buoyant bait over bottoms of soft silt or leaf and weed debris.

HOW TO SET UP THE RIG

Thread a float stop on to the line, followed by a bead, a swivel, another bead and another float stop.

A leger is tied to the end of the main line and a short stiff hair rig hook link is tied to the swivel.

Push the float stops, beads and swivel together to lock everything in place far enough up the line to ensure that the bait is not pulled below the silt and surface debris.

ZIG RIG

A rig to fish a buoyant bait above the bottom of the water that can be fished at any depth all the way up to the surface.

> **HOW TO SET UP THE RIG**
>
> Slide a float stop, bead and leger weight on to the main line followed by another rig bead and float stop.
>
> Tie a swivel to the end of the main line and complete the rig by tying a hair rig hook link to the swivel.

There are many ways to tie a zig rig, but to ensure maximum flexibility with this method you need to be able to vary the distance above the bottom that the bait is suspended so you can react to changes in the depth the carp are feeding at during a session.

A simple version of the zig rig based on the running leger rig can be constructed by the addition of float stops to regulate the fishing depth.

Use a buoyant bait with this rig such as a large popup boilie.

The depth at which the bait is fished can be adjusted by sliding the float stops, bead and hook link swivel up or down the line.

METHOD FEEDER RIG

A rig designed to allow a hook bait to be fished among a mix of ground bait and loose feed. It works best on well stocked waters where carp will compete for food.

> ### HOW TO SET UP THE RIG
>
> Thread one or two floats stops on to the line, followed by the feeder and tie a swivel to the end of the main line.
>
> Tie a very short hook link of about 3 inches (8 cm) to the other end of the swivel and push the float stop up to the feeder to lock everything in place.

A hard core of groundbait is moulded on to the feeder frame and the baited hook is pushed into the edge of this layer. A softer layer of groundbait containing samples of the hook bait is then moulded around the feeder.

When the feeder reaches the bottom, the groundbait will begin to break up, much like a ball of ground bait. On heavily stocked waters carp will attack the ball and eat anything that is dislodged, including your hook bait.

Many special 'method mix' ground baits have been developed for this method and you should find a good selection available at your local tackle shop.

PAUL DUFFIELD

RIVER FISHING

Rivers are varied habitats requiring different techniques depending on depth, width and speed of flow.

COMMON SPECIES
- Barbel
- Bream
- Chub
- Dace
- Perch
- Pike
- Roach

A quiet approach is recommended when fishing all rivers, but the smaller more intimate rivers require the most stealth when targeting shy and elusive fish such as large chub.

Mixed bags of primarily roach and dace can be caught with small baits on simple running water floats such as a stick, balsa or Avon on most medium to fast flowing rivers.

Larger specimens of barbel and chub will often be caught on larger baits fished using leger or swimfeeder tactics.

Very slow and deep rivers require a similar approach to still waters and can be fished using waggler floats.

GETTING STARTED IN COARSE FISHING

LOCATING FISH IN RIVERS

61

FLOAT RIGS FOR RIVERS

STICK FLOAT RIG

A rig for medium paced rivers up to 7 feet deep.

HOW TO SET UP THE RIG

The float is attached to the line using two pieces of silicon tubing. For wire stemmed stick floats a third piece of tubing is used at the base of the balsa body.

The shot required to set the float is made up of several shots, size 4, 6 or 8 depending on the capacity of the float, spaced evenly down the line.

The float should be allowed to travel through the swim at the speed of the current. Mend the line as necessary to keep a straight line to the float so it is not dragged or pulled out of position by the current.

Bites can sometimes be induced by holding back the float momentarily from time to time so the bait lifts in the water.

Bunch the shots together if a slower or faster falling bait is required.

DEEP WATER STICK FLOAT RIG

A rig for medium paced rivers over 7 feet deep.

> ### HOW TO SET UP THE RIG
>
> The float is attached to the line using two pieces of silicon tubing. For wire stemmed stick floats a third piece of tubing is used at the base of the balsa body.
>
> The shot required to set the float is made up of bunches of size 4, 6 or 8 shots depending on the capacity of the float, spaced evenly down the lower half of the line.

The float should be allowed to travel through the swim at the speed of the current. Mend the line as necessary to keep a straight line to the float so it is not dragged or pulled out of position by the current.

Bites can sometimes be induced by holding back the float momentarily from time to time so the bait lifts in the water.

BALSA FLOAT RIG

A rig for fast flowing rivers.

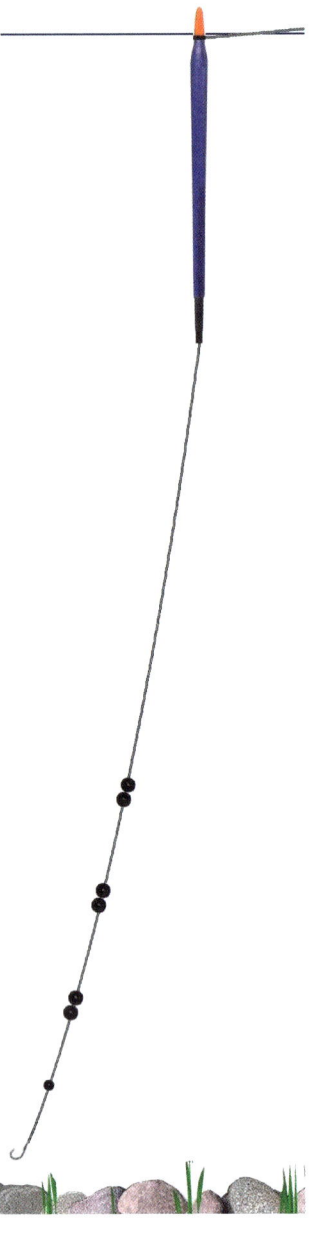

> **HOW TO SET UP THE RIG**
>
> The float is attached to the line using two pieces of silicon tubing.
>
> The shot required to set the float is made up of bunches of shots spaced evenly down the lower half of the line. Depending on the shot capacity of the float and the speed of the current, quite large shots, up to number 1 or BB may be required.

For very fast flows where the fish are feeding very close to the bottom, it may be necessary to bunch all of the shots together a few inches above the dropper shot.

The float should be controlled through the swim usually at the speed of the current, but it can sometimes be effective to release line under tension so the float travels slightly slower.

Mend the line as necessary to keep a straight line to the float so it is not dragged or pulled out of position by the current.

AVON FLOAT RIG

A rig for fishing at close to medium range in deep rivers with a medium to fast flow.

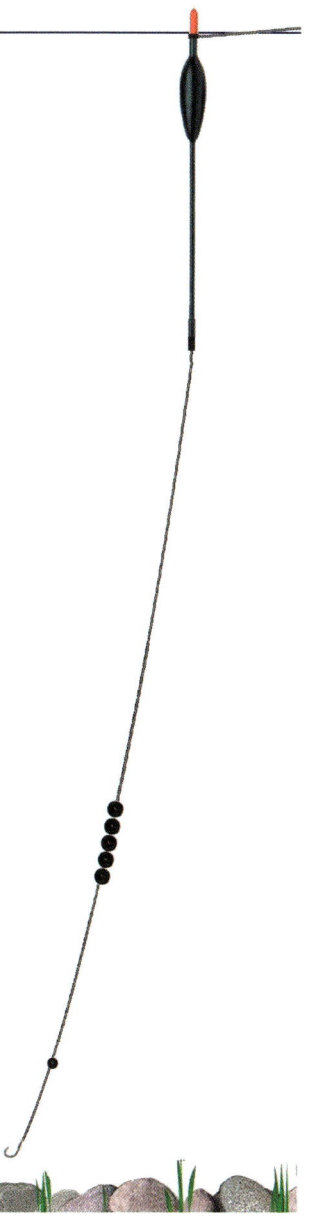

> **HOW TO SET UP THE RIG**
>
> The float is attached to the line using three pieces of silicon tubing placed at the top and bottom of the float and just below the body.
>
> Shotting consists of a bunch of large shot, AAA or BB depending on the shotting capacity of the float about 2 feet (30 cm) from the hook, and a smaller dropper shot.

On entering the water, the bulk of large shot will quickly take the hook bait to the bottom and the float is them allowed to move through the swim at the speed of the current.

Mend the line as necessary to keep a straight line to the float so it is not dragged or pulled out of position by the current.

Bites can sometimes be induced by slowing down the float or holding it back momentarily from time to time so the bait lifts in the water.

CHUBBER FLOAT RIG

A rig for fishing fast flowing shallow rivers with large baits such as worms and bread.

> ### HOW TO SET UP THE RIG
>
> The float is attached to the line using two pieces of silicon tubing.
>
> The shot required to set the float is made up of a single bunch of large shot, AAA or SSG depending on the shot carrying capacity of the float, with a single dropper, number 4 or number 6, near the hook.

The float should be controlled through the swim usually at the speed of the current, but it can sometimes be effective to release line under tension so the float travels slightly slower.

Mend the line as necessary to keep a straight line to the float so it is not dragged or pulled out of position by the current.

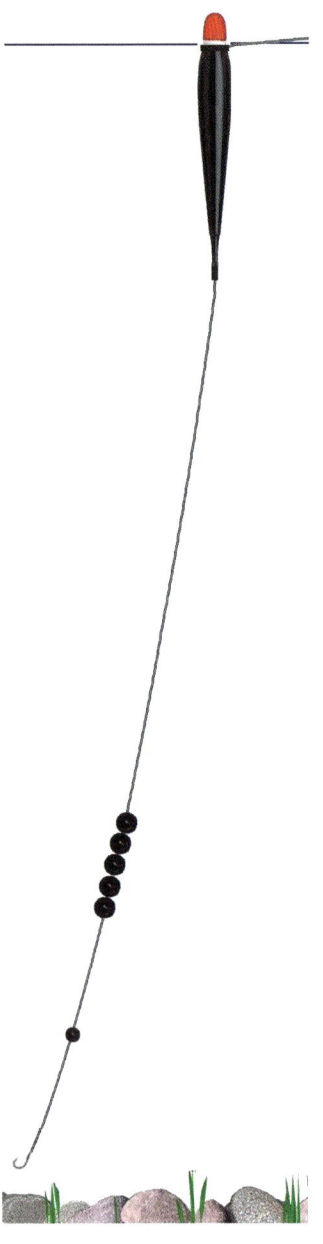

STRAIGHT WAGGLER FLOAT RIG

A rig for medium to fast flowing rivers where a downstream wind prevents use of a stick float.

HOW TO SET UP THE RIG

Most of the shot required to set the float is used to lock it on the line at the base.

The remaining shot is made up of number 6 or number 8 shots spaced evenly down the line, one shot for every two feet of depth, plus a number 8 dropper shot.

The float needs to travel through the swim naturally at the speed of the current, but the technique of mending the line used with floats attached top and bottom would drag the float under.

Instead, allow a bow to form between the rod tip and float and feed the bow by paying out enough line to allow the float to move unhindered down the swim.

A powerful strike is required with this method as you have to recover all of the line in the bow before making contact with the fish.

SPECI-WAGGLER FLOAT RIG

A rig for medium to fast flowing rivers where a long cast is required.

> ### HOW TO SET UP THE RIG
>
> Most of the shot required to set the float is used to lock it on the line at the base.
>
> The remaining shot is made up of number 4 shots spaced evenly down the line, one shot for every two feet of depth, plus a number 6 dropper shot.

The float needs to travel through the swim naturally at the speed of the current. Due to the extra thickness and buoyancy of this float, mending the line is usually possible without moving the float out of position.

If conditions make mending the line difficult on the day, allow a bow to form between the rod tip and float and feed the bow by paying out enough line to allow the float to move unhindered down the swim. .

LEGER AND SWIMFEEDER RIGS FOR RIVERS

RUNNING LEGER/FEEDER RIG

A simple rig for use with a leger or swimfeeder.

HOW TO SET UP THE RIG

Slide a link swivel on to the main line followed by a leger stop (a small split shot or swivel and bead can be used if you prefer), tie a loop in the main line and attach a hook link of 18 inches (45 cm).

A leger weight or swimfeeder is attached to the rig using the link swivel which gives you the flexibility to switch between leger or feeder, or change to a heavier or lighter leger weight without having to break the rig down.

As the line can pass freely through the eye of the swivel there is little resistance when a fish takes the bait.

SEMI-FIXED LEGER/FEEDER RIG

A semi-fixed version of the running leger rig. It can be very effective when bites are difficult to see because the fish are not moving far after taking your bait.

> HOW TO SET UP THE RIG
>
> Slide one or two float stops on to the main line, followed by a link swivel and a leger stop (a small split shot or swivel and bead can be used if you prefer), tie a loop in the main line and attach a hook link of 18 inches (45 cm).

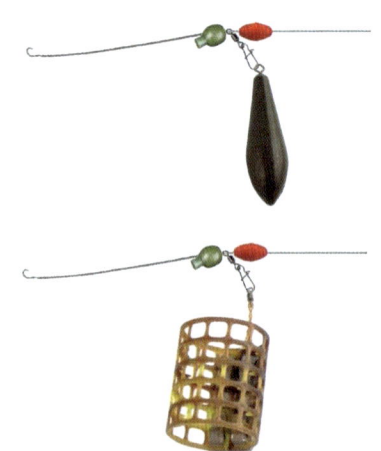

This rig is designed to provide resistance as soon as a fish takes the bait causing it to either swim away quickly and provide a positive indication of a bite, or hook itself against the weight of the leger or feeder.

PATERNOSTER FEEDER RIG

A very sensitive rig that shows up bites very well as any movement of the hook is quickly transmitted up the line to the rod tip.

HOW TO SET UP THE RIG

Slide one or two float stops on to the main line followed by swivel and a soft bead. Tie another swivel to the end of the main line and attach 10 inches (25 cm) of line to the other end of the swivel.

The leger or swimfeeder is tied to the end of this line and an 18 inch (45 cm) hook link is attached to the swivel between the bead and the float stop. Use the float stop to lock the hook length swivel in place.

Experiment with longer or shorter hook links if you have difficulty seeing or hitting bites.

INLINE FEEDER RIG

A semi-fixed rig, designed to provide resistance as soon as a fish takes the bait causing it to either swim away quickly and provide a positive indication of a bite, or hook itself against the weight of the feeder.

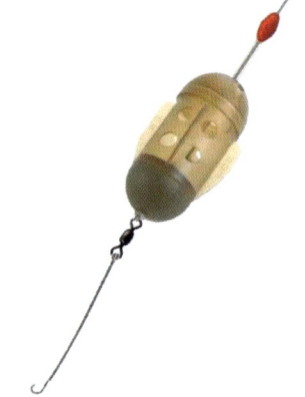

HOW TO SET UP THE RIG

Thread one or two floats stops on to the line, followed by the feeder and tie a swivel to the end of the main line.

Tie a very short hook link of about 3 inches (8 cm) to the other end of the swivel and push the float stop up to the feeder to lock everything in place.

The combination of a very short hook link and inline feeder makes this a very easy rig to cast quite long distances without tangles.

The reason for the short hook link is twofold. Firstly it ensures that your hook bait is among the maggots escaping from the feeder.

Secondly, it means that a fish will feel the resistance of the swimfeeder as soon as they take the bait which should result in a positive bite or hooked fish.

LINK LEGER RIG

A versatile rig designed to be used on rivers where there are overhanging trees, snags and rafts of weed.

HOW TO SET UP THE RIG

Slide a swivel on to the main line followed by a leger stop (a small split shot or swivel and bead can be used if you prefer).

Tie a loop in the main line and attach a hook link of 18 inches (45 cm).

The weight for this rig is added by passing a short length of line through the eye of the swivel, folding it to form a loop and attaching shot to lock it in place.

You should only add as much shot as is needed to just hold bottom against the current and if conditions change or you move swim you should adjust the shot accordingly.

This rig can be fished like a standard running leger rig, but if no bites are forthcoming, gently raising the rod to disturb the rig will lift it off the bottom and allow you to search the swim by drifting the rig further downstream or under overhanging branches.

FISHING FOR PREDATORY FISH

While small perch and zander and occasionally pike will be caught using general coarse fishing tactics, more specialised methods are needed to target the larger specimens.

TARGET SPECIES

- PERCH
- PIKE
- ZANDER

Artificial baits are popular for pike and perch fishing and all predatory species can be targeted with fish baits.

Live baits where allowed will catch all three species. Pike and zander will both take dead freshwater baits and dead sea fish are a popular bait for pike.

DEAD BAITS

Dead baits are usually attached using a wire trace with two sets of treble hooks, one located at the end of the trace, the other set a short distance back.

The treble hook that is located along the trace should be pushed firmly into the tail root of the dead bait as this hook will bear the force of the cast.

The treble hook positioned at the end of the trace should be lightly hooked into the flesh on the back or side of the dead bait.

If you are using rigs with semi-barbed treble hooks, i.e. two of the points are barbless, insert the barbed points into the dead bait as these will grip the bait much more firmly.

LIVE BAITS

In recent years live baiting has become a controversial subject with some clubs and fisheries banning their use and others imposing rules controlling which rigs can be used.

Where it is allowed, live baits can be hooked in the same way as dead baits using a wire trace with two treble hooks.

An alternative is to use a wire trace terminated by one treble hook and hooking the live bait through one lip using one hook of the treble.

If treble hooks are not allowed on the water you intend to fish, the live bait can be hooked through one lip using a large single hook attached to a wire trace.

Before using live baits or any of these rigs, check the rules of your club or fishery to make sure that they are allowed.

ARTIFICIAL BAITS

A technique known as spinning where an artificial bait designed to imitate a prey fish is cast out and retrieved is a popular method for targeting pike and perch. The different types of lures used are explained in the section on bait later in this book.

In recent years, a technique widely used in America called drop shotting has become popular in the U.K. especially on canals which contain large populations of perch, zander and pike.

PAUL DUFFIELD

RIGS FOR PREDATOR FISHING

INLINE FLOAT RIG

A versatile rig that can be used on still waters and rivers with both live and dead baits.

> ### HOW TO SET UP THE RIG
>
> Slide a float stop on to the main line (omit this step if you prefer to use a stop knot), followed by a rig bead.
>
> Tie the end of the main line to a pike trace of 2 feet (60 cm) in length and attach enough SSG shot at the top of the trace to cock the float.

Use less shot to allow for the weight of the bait if you intend to fish with the bait suspended off the bottom.

This rig can be fished on or above the bottom to drift or move with the current or with the float set over depth to present a semi-static bait on still and slow moving water.

PENCIL SLIDER FLOAT LEGER RIG

A rig for legering a dead bait close in or at range.

HOW TO SET UP THE RIG

Slide a float stop on to the main line (omit this step if you prefer to use a stop knot), followed by a rig bead.

Slide on the float followed by another rig bead.

Tie the end of the main line to a pike trace of 2 feet (60 cm) in length.

Attach enough SSG shot at the top of the trace to anchor the bait.

PATERNOSTER FLOAT LEGER RIG

A rig to suspend a bait off the bottom or on top of a bed of weed or sit.

HOW TO SET UP THE RIG

Slide a float stop on to the main line (omit this step if you prefer to use a stop knot), followed by a rig bead.

Slide on the float followed by another rig bead.

Tie the end of the main line to a swivel and attach a length of line suitable for the depth at which you want to suspend the bait to the other ring of the swivel.

To complete the rig, attach a pike trace to the top eye using a link swivel.

Use line weaker than the main line with overhand knots tied in it for the leger link. This is often referred to as a 'rotten bottom'.

The leger will break off if it becomes snagged while playing a fish and allows the fish to lose the lead if the line breaks above the swivel.

GETTING STARTED IN COARSE FISHING

PATERNOSTER LEGER RIG

A rig for long range fishing when you need to suspend a bait off the bottom or on top of a bed of weed or silt.

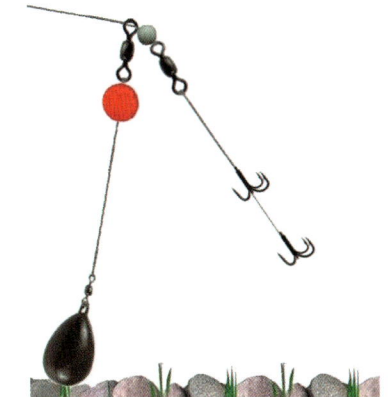

HOW TO SET UP THE RIG

Slide a swivel on to the main line, followed by a bead and tie the end of the main line to a pike trace.

Attach a length of line suitable for the depth at which you want to suspend the bait to the other ring of the swivel.

Attach a foam bait suspender (known as poppers and polyballs) to this line and tie a leger to the other end.

There is no risk of the fish being attached to the leger in the event of a break, but if a weaker line is used for the leger link it will break off if it becomes snagged when playing a fish.

POPPED UP LEGER RIG

A rig to fish a floating bait off the bottom.

HOW TO SET UP THE RIG

Slide a swivel on to the main line, followed by a bead and tie the end of the main line to a pike trace with bait suspenders (known as poppers and polyballs) attached to suspend the bait.

Attach 2 feet (60 cm) of to the other ring of the swivel and tie a leger to the other end.

There is no risk of the fish being attached to the leger in the event of a break, but if a weaker line is used for the leger link it will break off if it becomes snagged when playing a fish.

DROP SHOT RIG

A rig for fishing soft artificial lures and worms to catch perch.

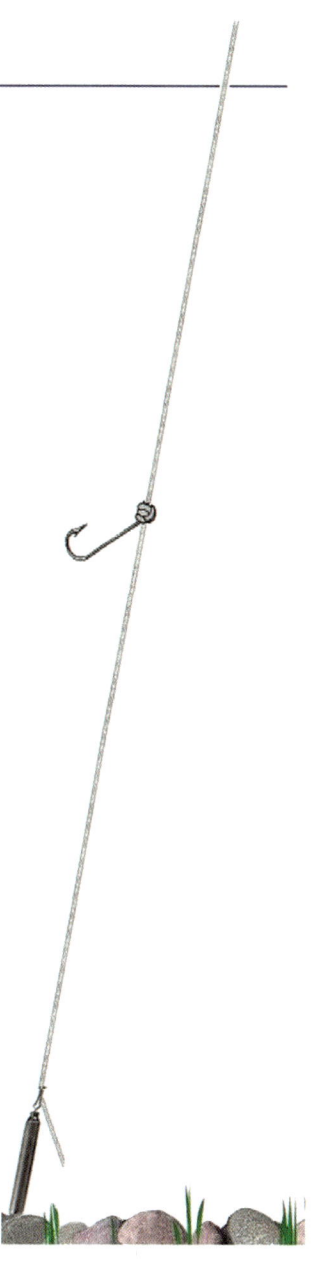

HOW TO SET UP THE RIG

Using a Palomar knot, tie the hook directly to the main line 18 inches from the end of the line ensuring that the hook points upwards.

Attach a drop shot weight to the end of the main line.

The drop shot rig can be used with soft artificial lures such as shads and with live worms.

The drop shot weight can be moved up and down the main line to alter the depth at which the bait is fished.

After casting, the tip of the rod is moved to impart movement to the lure to induce a take.

PAUL DUFFIELD

KNOW YOUR COARSE FISH

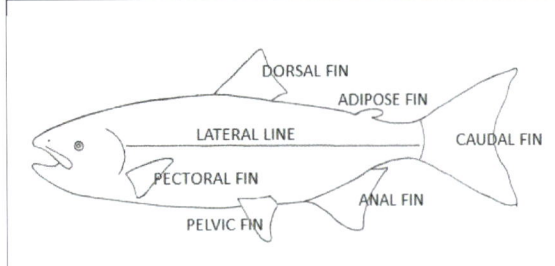

ANATOMY

Coarse fish anatomy is shown in the illustration on the left. Some species (bullhead, perch and zander) have two dorsal fins. The grayling is the only coarse fish that has an adipose fin.

SPECIES IDENTIFICATION

BARBEL	BLEAK	BREAM (BRONZE)	BREAM (SILVER)	BULLHEAD
CARP (COMMON)	CARP (CRUCIAN)	CARP (GRASS)	CARP (LEATHER)	CARP (MIRROR)
CATFISH (WELS)	CHUB	DACE	EEL	GRAYLING
GUDGEON	HYBRID (BREAM-RUDD)	HYBRID (ROACH-BREAM)	LOACH	MINNOW
ORFE (GOLDEN)	PERCH	PIKE	ROACH	RUDD
RUFFE	STICKLEBACK	TENCH	ZANDER	

82

BARBEL

Barbus barbus

A long bodied fish with a prominent snout flanked on each side by two barbels.

WHERE TO FIND THEM

While barbel have been stocked in some still water fisheries, they are primarily a river fish and can be found in many river systems.

HOW TO FISH FOR THEM

Both float and leger tactics can be used to catch barbel, but in faster flowing rivers, legering is usually a more productive method.

On small rivers a bed of loose feed can be introduced by hand and a bait fished over the top using a running leger rig, but on larger rivers, a swimfeeder approach will work best.

On small rivers that hold isolated populations of large barbel, a stalking approach to target individual fish can be productive.

BREAM

Abramis brama

A deep bodied fish that is relatively thin across the body.

Young bream have silver flanks, changing to bronze in the larger specimens.

WHERE TO FIND THEM

Large bream are found over silt beds in the deeper areas of still waters and the slower deeper reaches of rivers.

HOW TO FISH FOR THEM

Legering using a groundbait feeder with a sensitive quivertip is a popular method for larger specimens.

Small still water bream can be caught with waggler float tackle.

SILVER BREAM *Blicca bjoernika*

A separate less common species, mature silver bream retain their silver colouration.

They are less widespread and do not grow as large as common bream.

CARP

Cyprinus carpio

A deep bodied fish with large scales, two barbels and a large dorsal fin.

WHERE TO FIND THEM

Following extensive stocking, carp are one of the most widespread and commonly caught fish.

They can be found in all types of waters and large numbers of carp from a few pounds to low double figures can be caught in many still water commercial fisheries.

Larger specimens can be found in specialised carp fisheries, canals and the slower parts of rivers.

HOW TO FISH FOR THEM

Smaller carp can be caught using waggler, pole and leger tactics in commercial still waters. Larger specimens require a different approach using specialised carp rigs.

SCALE VARIATIONS

Mirror, leather and common carp are all the same species.

Mirror carp have patches of large scales, leather carp have very few or no scales.

CATFISH

Silurus glanis

A powerful fish with a large mouth flanked by 6 barbels.

WHERE TO FIND THEM

Catfish are found primarily in still water fisheries where they have been deliberately stocked.

HOW TO FISH FOR THEM

Catfish are usually targeted with leger tactics. Favourite baits are dead baits, shrimp and squid. Fishmeal boilies have also been known to catch catfish.

CHUB

Leuciscus cephalus

A thick set fish with a large mouth and dark edged scales.

WHERE TO FIND THEM

Chub are mainly present in medium and fast flowing rivers.

HOW TO FISH FOR THEM

Float and leger tactics will both catch chub, but a roving approach is usually best for catching chub in small and medium sized rivers. A leger rig using just enough weight to hold bottom should be cast into any likely spot near bushes or trees in the deeper parts of the river.

Chub will take almost any bait, including maggots and worms where there are not too many smaller fish to take the bait first, but firm favourites are bread in all its forms and cheese either used on its own or mixed with breadcrumbs to make a strongly flavoured paste.

CRUCIAN CARP

Carassius carassius

A deep bodied stocky fish with a blunt head and bronze flanks.

WHERE TO FIND THEM

Primarily a still water fish, the crucian carp is found in many pools and small lakes. Some rivers and canals also hold small populations.

HOW TO FISH FOR THEM

Crucian Carp will take most baits including maggots, bread, worms, sweetcorn and pellets presented using light float tactics.

DACE

Leuciscus leuciscus

Slim silver fish that are very similar in appearance to small chub.

WHERE TO FIND THEM

Dace are widely distributed but prefer fast flowing water so are mostly found in rivers although there are small populations of dace in some still waters.

HOW TO FISH FOR THEM

Dace are generally fished for with using small baits such as maggots and small pieces of bread but larger specimens can be caught using bread flake, paste and worms.

Light float fishing methods on rivers will account for dace where they will often be caught as part of a mixed bag with roach.

EEL

Anguilla anguilla

A snake like fish with a small head and long dorsal fin.

WHERE TO FIND THEM

The eel is widely distributed throughout British waters, but is most commonly encountered in larger numbers in slow flowing rivers and drains.

HOW TO FISH FOR THEM

Eels will take most live baits used by anglers such as maggots and worms. Larger specimens will take dead baits of whole or sectioned coarse and sea fish.

Large eels are usually fished for with leger tackle using dead baits or bunches of large worms.

GRAYLING

Thymallus thymallus

A silver coloured fish with a large sail shaped dorsal fin and an adipose fin between the dorsal fin and the tail.

WHERE TO FIND THEM

In rivers where they are present, grayling will generally be found in the faster parts of rivers.

HOW TO FISH FOR THEM

Float fishing with maggots is a good method for catching grayling, but they will also take legered baits.

Fly fishing is also a popular method for catching grayling and they will take both dry (floating) and wet (sinking) flies.

GUDGEON

Gobio gobio

A small elongate round bodied fish with two barbels.

WHERE TO FIND THEM

Some canals have very large populations of gudgeon, but the larger specimens are to be found in rivers where they are often caught by anglers targeting other species such as roach and dace.

HOW TO FISH FOR THEM

Maggots, especially pinkies are a good bait for gudgeon.

Fishing close in with a small whip on canals is an effective method for catching gudgeon.

Small amounts of loose feed and groundbait should be fed regularly to keep the gudgeon in the swim and feeding.

ORFE

Leuciscus idus

Golden coloured slender and streamlined fish with large tails.

WHERE TO FIND THEM

Orfe are stocked in many still water commercial fisheries.

HOW TO FISH FOR THEM

General float fishing tactics with most baits will catch orfe. They can also sometimes be caught with floating baits.

PERCH

Perca fluviatilis

A very distinctive fish with a large spiked dorsal fin and striped flanks.

WHERE TO FIND THEM

Populations of perch exist in most British waters. Small Perch live in shoals, whilst the largest specimens tend to be solitary.

HOW TO FISH FOR THEM

Small perch can be taken with most float fishing and legering methods where they will often make up part of a mixed bag.

Where large perch are known to be present they can be caught using small artificial spinners. In recent years, drop shotting has become a popular method for targeting perch, especially in canals.

Legering with large worms such as lobs and dendrobaenas is also a good technique that can account for quite large perch.

GETTING STARTED IN COARSE FISHING

PIKE

Esox lucius

A long slim fish with a large mouth and green/brown camouflage markings on the flanks.

WHERE TO FIND THEM

Pike are widespread throughout British waters and will generally be found where there is cover that will hide them from their prey.

HOW TO FISH FOR THEM

Pike can be caught with lures as well as live fresh water fish and both fresh water and sea fish dead baits.

ROACH

Rutilus Rutilus

A moderately deep bodied fish with silver flanks and red fins.

WHERE TO FIND THEM

Roach are widespread throughout British waters and can be found in shoals in still, slow moving and fast moving water.

HOW TO FISH FOR THEM

Most coarse fishing tactics will catch roach depending on the type of water and conditions.

In rivers they can be fished for with light tackle by trotting a stick float with the stream, using maggots or casters.

Larger river specimens can be taken using a leger or swimfeeder rig, with larger baits such as worm, bread flake or paste allowing selective targeting of the larger specimens.

In ponds, lakes and canals, pole or whip tactics can account for large bags of small or medium sized roach using pinkies or maggots with a cloud groundbait.

RUDD

Scardinius erythrophthalmus

A moderately deep bodied fish with bronze flanks and deep red fins.

WHERE TO FIND THEM

Rudd are widely distributed throughout British still water coarse fisheries such as ponds, lakes and canals as well as slow moving rivers.

HOW TO FISH FOR THEM

Like roach, rudd are generally fished for with small baits such as maggots or pellets, with bread flake or paste being a popular bait for the larger specimens. They will also take worms and small boilies.

Rudd can also be taken from the surface with floating breadflake, and they will also take an artificial fly presented with fly tackle.

TENCH

Tinca tinca

A thick set fish with a rounded body and small dark olive green scales.

WHERE TO FIND THEM

Tench are present in many lakes, ponds and canals as well as the slower reaches of rivers.

They like to inhabit thick vegetation and will often be found in marginal areas among lily pads and thick weed beds.

HOW TO FISH FOR THEM

Tench are bottom feeders. Float tackle set to present the bait on the bottom is a popular and successful method.

They will take most popular baits including maggots, worms, sweetcorn, pellets, bread and small boilies.

The best times to fish for tench are early mornings just after dawn and in the last hours of daylight.

Large patches of bubbles rising to the surface are a sure indication that feeding tench are present in a swim.

ZANDER

Stizostedion lucioperca

A long bodied fish with a small head and two dorsal fins, the fin nearest the head having spikes similar to perch.

WHERE TO FIND THEM

Whilst not as widely distributed as either the Pike or the Perch, large populations exist in some rivers and canals.

HOW TO FISH FOR THEM

Live baits, where allowed, will account for zander either fished under a heavy float and allowed to swim freely, or on a paternoster float-leger rig. Most coarse fish are suitable as live bait, but the practice is not always allowed.

Where live baiting is not permitted, Zander can also be taken on fresh water dead baits as well as artificial lures.

OTHER SPECIES

There are several other species of coarse fish that, while you do not set out specifically to catch them, may take baits intended for other species.

BLEAK

Alburnus alburnus

The Bleak is a small silver fish that is mostly found in rivers.

A shoal fish, large numbers of them can be found near the surface where they will often intercept baits intended for other species.

BULLHEAD

Cottus Gobio

A river fish, also known as the Millers Thumb, the bullhead is a small fish with a large flattened head that will sometimes take maggots or worms intended for other species.

LOACH

Cobitis taenia (Spined Loach), Noemacheilus barbatulus (Stone Loach)

Two species of loach are found in British waters; the Spined Loach and the Stone Loach. Both varieties have barbels, those on the spined loach being smaller.

Usually not exceeding a few inches in length, loach are rarely caught on rod and line, but may take small maggots or worms.

MINNOW

Phoxinus phoxinus

The minnow is a very small fish with dark markings along the flank. It has quite a blunt snout and very small scales.

Where present in large numbers they are often regarded as a nuisance fish. They are bold feeders and readily attack baits intended for other species.

RUFFE

Gymnocephalus cernua

The ruffe is similar in appearance to the perch, but with drab colouration. They do not grow to a large size, and although they are quite widespread they are not usually found in large numbers.

Where present, they will take small baits such as maggots and worms.

STICKLEBACK

Gasterosteus aculeatus (Three Spined), Pungitius pungitius (Ten Spined)

Easily recognisable, and possibly the best known British freshwater fish, these fish have three or ten spines along the back before the dorsal fin.

The three spined stickleback is the more common and is found everywhere from small ditches to rivers and lakes. The ten spined stickleback is more rare, and is found in stagnant waters in mud and weed.

They may occasionally be caught by anglers fishing with maggots or worms.

PAUL DUFFIELD

KNOW YOUR BAITS

POPULAR COARSE FISHING BAITS

Bread	Bread is a very versatile bait that will catch most species. It can be cut into cubes, flake from the middle of a loaf can be pressed on to the shank of a hook and crust can be used as a floating bait.	
Boilies	Boilies will catch fish of a variety of species. They are available in a wide range of sizes, colours and flavours. Smaller boilies in savoury flavours are a good river bait for chub and barbel.	
Cheese	Hard cheese, such as cheddar can be kneaded until soft and moulded around a hook. This is a popular bait for chub, but will catch other species too. As an alternative, flavour bread paste with cheese by adding it at the kneading stage.	
Groundbait	Groundbait will attract fish into the swim and keep them there while they forage for food. It is particularly effective for keeping a shoal of bream feeding in slow moving rivers and still waters.	

GETTING STARTED IN COARSE FISHING

Hemp seed	Hemp seed is a good summer bait for roach. It can be used as loose feed with either a grain of hemp or a tare on the hook. It is also a good feed bait for holding barbel in a swim when fishing larger baits such as luncheon meat on the hook.
Luncheon meat	Luncheon meat is a popular bait for barbel and chub. It can be cut into cubes, pressed into cylinders using a bait punch, cut into thin slices or torn from the block.
Maggots	Maggots were once the most popular bait for coarse fishing and are still a very effective bait for all species. Casters, the chrysalis form of the maggot is a also a good bait and can sometimes pick out the larger fish in a shoal.
Paste	Bread paste is an excellent roach bait and with the addition of flavours such as cheese is also good for chub and barbel. Commercially available prepared paste baits will catch fish of most species. 
Pellets	Small soft pellets are a good alternative to maggots in still waters and rivers. Larger pellets fished on a hair rig or attached to the hook with a bait band will catch bream, carp chub and barbel. 

Sweetcorn	Sweetcorn can be used straight from the tin in its natural yellow form and is a good bait for many species. Flavoured and coloured sweetcorn for fishing is available in many tackle shops.	
Worms	Worms are an excellent bait for most species. Larger varieties such as lobworms and dendrobaenas are good baits for chub and perch while smaller varieties such as redworms will be taken by fish of all species.	

ARTIFICIAL BAITS

There is an artificial version for just about every kind of hook bait including maggots, worms, sweetcorn, dog biscuits, pellets, boilies and bread.

Although they have no nutritional value and cannot be digested, they can be very successful when fished over a bed of feed. Some anglers flavour artificial baits to increase their attractiveness.

Floating artificial baits can be fished on a hair alongside real baits to make them buoyant, for example you could fish a floating grain of artificial sweetcorn between two real grains of sweetcorn on a hair rig.

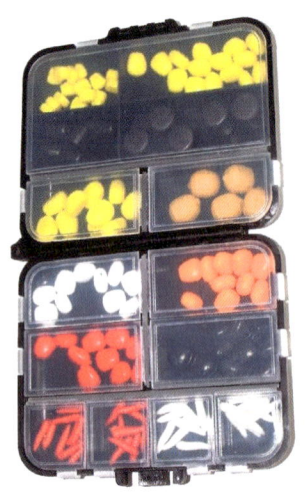

GETTING STARTED IN COARSE FISHING

LIVE AND DEAD BAITS

Live Baits	Small coarse fish such as Roach, Rudd, Bream, Gudgeon and Minnows are suitable for use when fishing for Pike, Perch or Zander.	
Dead Baits	Coarse fish can be used as dead baits for pike and zander. Sea fish such as sprats and mackerel can be used for pike, either whole or cut into strips or chunks.	

LURES

Spinners	Spinners have a blade which rotates around a central spindle when retrieved. Small spinners of the Mepps type shown are good for catching perch	
Spoons	Larger than spinners and without the central spindle, spoons are a good lure for pike and zander.	

Plugs	Floating lures that have a vane incorporated near the head which causes them to dive below the surface when retrieved.	
Poppers	Similar to plugs, but with a concave head designed to maximise disturbance and prevent the lure from diving below the surface.	
Shads	Soft fish shaped lures that are mainly used with a drop shot rig to catch perch.	
Jelly Lures	Soft lures made of silicon, similar to shads, but incorporating hooks and casting weight. The larger sizes can be used for pike and zander and the smaller ones for perch.	

USEFUL KNOTS

KNOTS FOR MAKING LOOPS

BLOOD LOOP KNOT

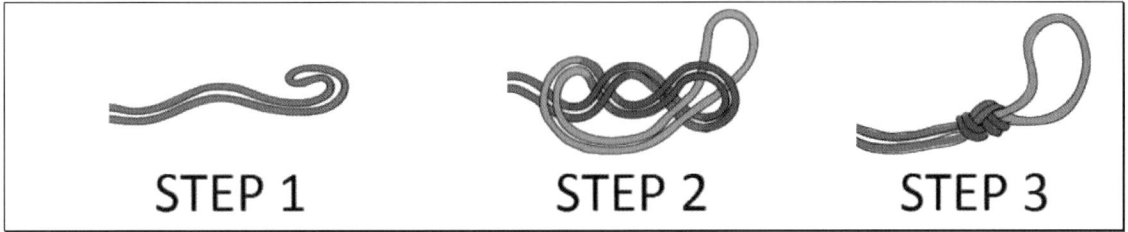

1. Double over the line to form a loop.
2. Twist the loop and pass the doubled end of the line back through the first loop.
3. Moisten the knot, pull tight and trim.

SURGEON'S LOOP KNOT

1. Double the line back on itself to form a loop.
2. Form a loop using the doubled line and pass the end through this larger loop two or three times.
3. Moisten the knot, pull tight and trim.

KNOTS FOR JOINING LINE

LOOP METHOD

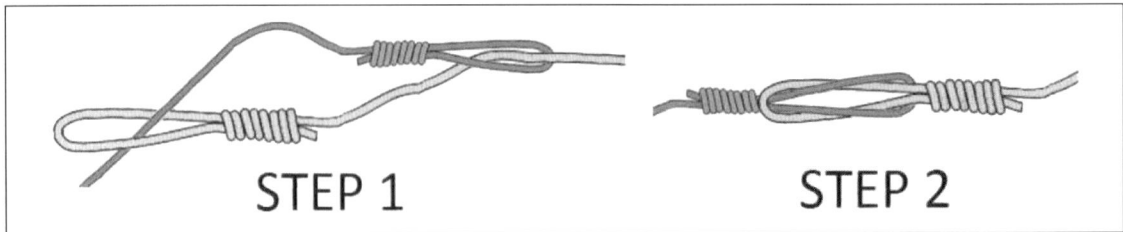

1. Tie a loop into the end of each line to be joined using either the surgeon's loop knot or a blood loop knot.
2. Thread the loops together as shown.
3. Pull tight.

BLOOD KNOT

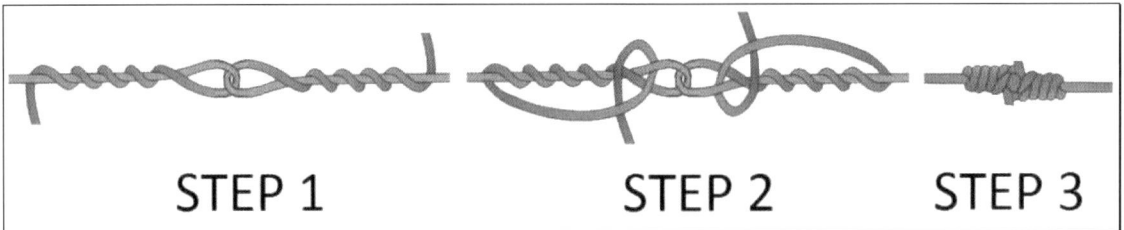

The blood knot is used to join lines of similar diameter.

1. Wrap one length of line around the other to form interlocked loops.
2. Twist both loops and pass the standing ends back through the loops where they connect.
3. Pass the standing ends through each of the loops.
4. Moisten the knot, pull tight and trim.

ALBRIGHT KNOT

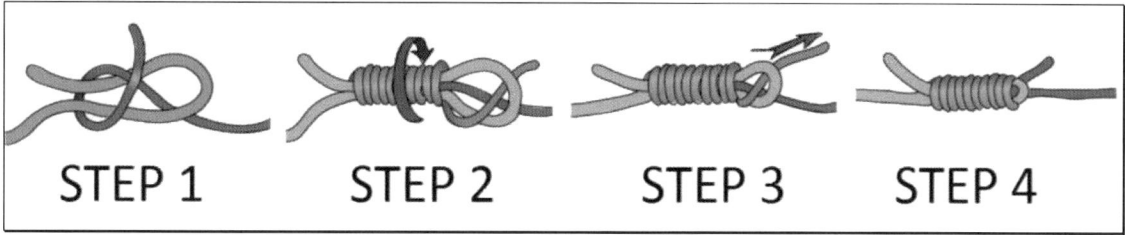

The Albright knot is used to join lines that are not of similar diameter.

1. Form a loop in the thicker of the two lines.
2. Pass the end of the thinner line through the loop and wrap it neatly around itself and the loop ten times.
3. Pass the end back through the loop so it exits on the same side it entered.
4. Moisten the knot, pull tight and trim.

KNOTS FOR HOOKS AND SWIVELS

SNELL KNOT

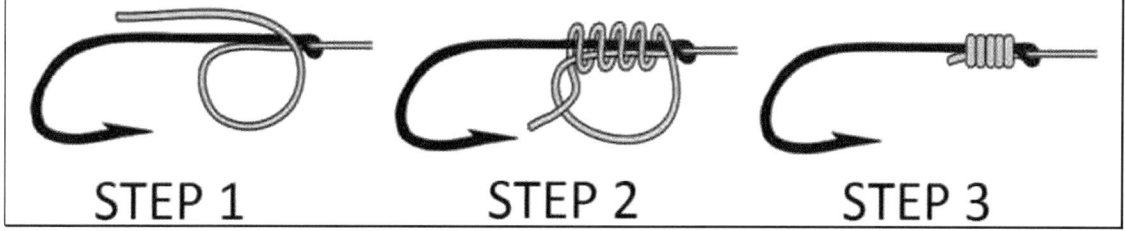

This knot can be used to tie either eyed or spade end hooks.

1. . Hold the line parallel to the hook shank.
2. Form a loop and pass the standing end of the line through the loop five or six times.
3. Moisten the knot, pull tight and trim.

THE KNOTLESS KNOT FOR HAIR RIGS

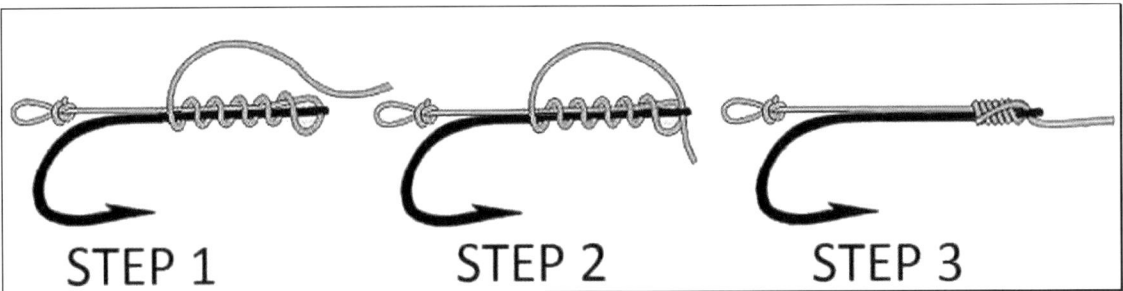

1. Tie a loop for the hair and pass the free end of the line through the eye of the hook.

2. Wrap the free end of the line back down the hook 8 to 10 times.

3. Pass the free end of the line back through the eye and pull tight.

THE PALOMAR KNOT FOR DROP SHOT RIGS

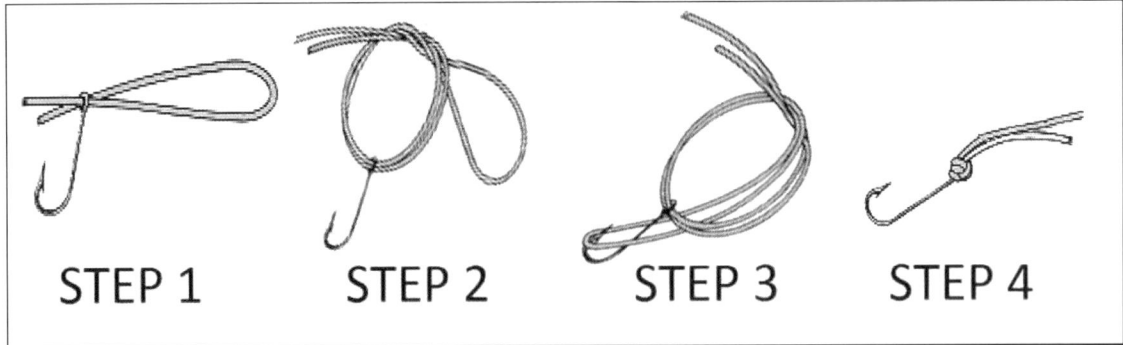

1. Form a loop in the line and pass it through the eye of the hook.

2. Tie an overhand knot in the doubled line.

3. Pull the loop back over the hook.

4. Tighten by pulling on both ends of the line.

OTHER KNOTS

STOP KNOT

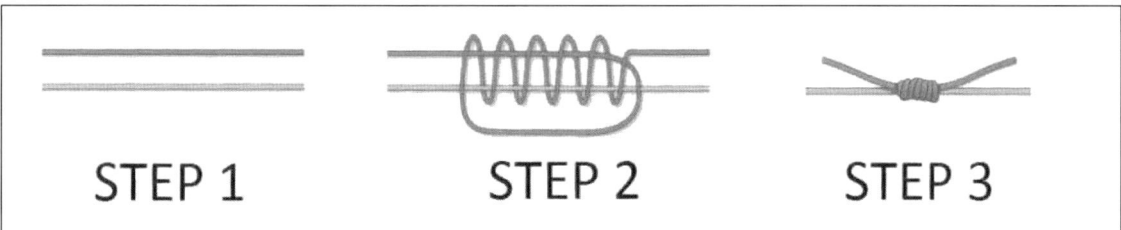

1. Hold the stop knot material to be used for the stop knot (e.g. line or powergum) parallel to the main line.

2. Fold the stop knot material to form a loop and wrap five turns around both the stop knot material and the main line inside the loop.

3. Moisten the knot, pull tight and trim.

ARBOR KNOT (to attach line or backing to a reel)

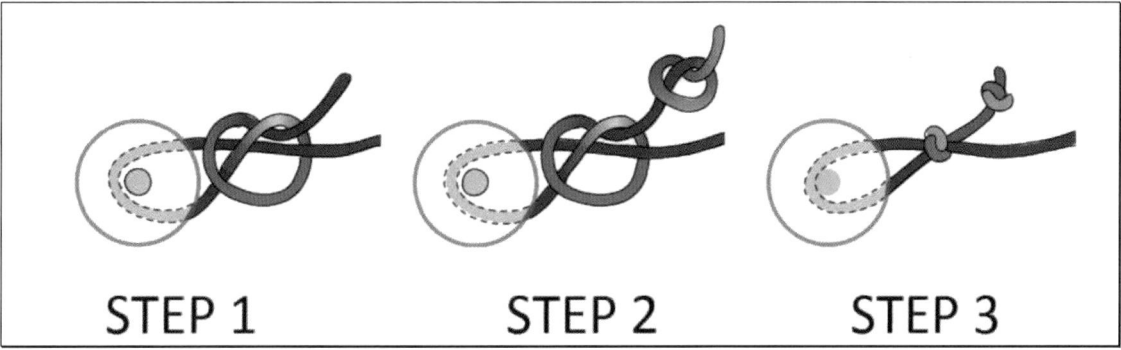

1. Pass the line or backing around the spool and tie an overhand knot around the free end of the line.

2. Tie a second overhand knot in the free end of the line to act as a stop.

3. Slide the knots down to the spool and pull tight.

LICENSES AND PERMISSION TO FISH

Anyone aged 12 or over must have a fishing licence to fish for salmon, trout, freshwater fish, smelt or eel with a rod and line in:

- England (except the River Tweed)
- Wales
- the Border Esk region of Scotland

You must always carry your rod fishing licence when you're fishing or you could be prosecuted. The penalty for being caught fishing without a licence is a fine of up to £2,500.

Full details of current prices can be found on the GOV.UK website where you can also apply for a licence:

https://www.gov.uk/fishing-licences/buy-a-fishing-licence

You can also buy a licence by calling the Environment Agency on 0344 800 5386 between 8am and 6pm, Monday to Friday and in person at a Post Office if the licence is for someone over 16.

A licence only allows you to fish legally, it does not mean you can fish anywhere you choose. There are some locations where you can fish for free, but most fishing waters are either owned by fishing clubs that you have to join, or available to fish by purchasing a day ticket.

On rivers there is an annual close season for coarse fishing from 15 March to 15 June each year and you are not allowed to fish using coarse fishing methods during that period.

There is no close season for coarse fishing on lakes, canals and ponds so you are legally allowed to fish all year round, but some clubs enforce their own close season, so check the rules for your chosen fishery before setting out.

GETTING STARTED IN COARSE FISHING

If you intend to fish at night, which can be a very productive time for many species, check with your local club or fishery to find out if this is allowed, and whether you need to obtain a special night fishing permit.

ABOUT THE AUTHOR

I was born in Oxford in 1959, but spent most of my childhood further north in the West Midlands. I am currently based in Devon in the south west of England, but still have a particular fondness for the Warwickshire and Worcestershire countryside.

I became interested in nature at a young age and spent a lot of my free time and holidays out in the fresh air walking and fishing with friends. I've lived, worked, walked and fished over many parts of Britain and that early interest has developed into a fascination for the natural world.

As well as writing, I collect and restore vintage fishing tackle and make traditional fishing floats. I like to fish with cane rods, centrepin reels and quill floats and when I'm not writing I like nothing more than to spend a few hours on a country stream fishing and watching birds, butterflies, and other wild creatures in their natural environment.

You can contact me using the contact form at my website below:

http://www.traditionalfishingfloats.co.uk

Details of other books I have written can be found on my Amazon author pages:

http://www.amazon.co.uk/Paul-Duffield/e/B00BEYO9PI/

Printed in Great Britain
by Amazon